Finally. . .

COMEDY
BY THE
NUMBERS©
VOLUME 1!*

*includes the equivalent of TWO volumes of comedy

As we all know, true creativity comes from simple formulas and the memorization of data. This new manual makes the secrets of comedy accessible, not only to those funny few among us, but also to those who might not have the ability or talent to be funny! Hey, maybe that's YOU!

We've used the tried and true form of "listing things" to make it easier on the "class clown" or "office cut-up" or even the "neighborhood nerd" to go from "dud to dude!"©

With the aid of this biblette, one no longer need worry about originality – just find the right comedy number and apply as needed to your situation… **and then you're on your way to popularityville!**©

Pretty soon you'll be hearing, "Nice #8, [your name]!"

Aren't you lucky you picked up this book?!?

Upper part of this page has been intentionally left blank in order to not distract
from important information about the publisher below.

MᶜSWEENEY'S BOOKS
SAN FRANCISCO

For more information about McSweeney's, see www.mcsweeneys.net

Copyright © 2007 Eric Hoffman and Gary Rudoren.

McSweeney's and colophon are registered trademarks of McSweeney's,
a privately held company with wildly fluctuating resources.

ISBN-13: 978-1-932416-75-6

Printed in Canada

This book is dedicated to
Dame Laughter,
our muse.

WELCOME TO THE FIRST PAGE OF THE REST OF YOUR LIFE!

AN OPEN LETTER TO OUR FRIEND, YOU, THE BOOK PURCHASER

Hey! Good to see you. We wanted to let you know that this is not only the first page of this book, but it's the first page of the rest of your life! (Please realize that we do know that the page previous to this, which had very large typeface and an introductory greeting that said "WELCOME TO THE FIRST PAGE OF THE REST OF YOUR LIFE," is really the first page. And even then we realize that it's probably not the actual first page, given the legal fillers and whatever dedication page we come up with. We know you get it, but we just really wanted to start the book off in a friendly manner, so you would like us right off the bat.)

HERE GOES!

A great man once said: "*The promise of laughter is the hope of the future.*" History doesn't name that man, but nonetheless, if that man were alive today, we're sure he would be endorsing **COMEDY BY THE NUMBERS**© as a reasonably priced solution to solving society's ills and your problems in particular.

WE KNOW THAT SOUNDS OUTLANDISH!

Don't get us wrong. We're not trying to be arrogant. We are merely simple, funny men who believe that Christians, Jews (see #63), Muslims, and people of ALL stereotypes can benefit from our book. We say, humbly, that if each and every person were to pick up a copy of COMEDY BY THE NUMBERS© and not only skim through it (we've all done that, haven't we?) but read it, embrace it, and memorize some of the bits – then, well, watch out world, "Somethin' funny's gonna happen!"© (And THEN, subsequently, after the funny happens – peace, prosperity, happiness, etc. will kick in.)

So we don't have to hope you like the book – we KNOW you will!

Your new friends,

Dr. Gary Rudoren
       Prof. Eric Hoffman

Dr. Gary Rudoren & Prof. Eric Hoffman

A CLARIFICATION

There is no doubt in our minds that if you read this book a few times, learn the numbers by heart, and fully inhale the comedy knowledge, hints, tips, etc. we have painstakingly assembled for you, then your life will reach heretofore undiscovered heights and you will be well on your way toward becoming the funniest version of yourself that you could ever hope to be. HOWEVER, we feel obliged to let you know that we purposefully did not include all the comedy secrets we know.

It makes sense, doesn't it? If we were to give you EVERYTHING in this ONE book, then we would leave ourselves no room for a sequel. Honestly, if this book doesn't sell, there won't be a sequel – we just don't have the energy or the time. HOWEVER, if this book DOES do well (financially, we mean, and possibly critically even), then we promise that we will put out another book called, probably, *MORE... COMEDY BY THE NUMBERS.*© Consider this a friendly warning: without that book, who knows what will happen to you? We're not bluffing either. As a matter of fact, we're bolding this next sentence because of its importance. **The financial reality of a sequel is entirely up to YOU, because unless you buy multiple copies of this book to give to people as "Hey, I saw this and thought of you" friend-gifts, we can't guarantee that you'll become truly popular and funny.** Our fate and your fate are intertwined, inside your wallet, even as we type. (We're also thinking about making some coin from mugs, T-shirts, and the lucrative page-a-day calendar market.)

Oh, also, be warned that there may be some cursing in this book.

SOMETHING ELSE WE SHOULD TELL YOU ABOUT

At the request of our lawyers, we would like to make a correction to the cover of this book. Unfortunately, due to a very tight printing schedule (and an unconscientiously lazy proofreader with personal problems) this error was not picked up until it was "too late." So we'd like to set the record straight: Gary Rudoren (formerly Gary Ruderman, but that's another book) is not, and never has been, a certified "Dr." of any type, nor has he ever received any honorariums or degrees from universities that bestow that sort of thing. He simply likes to refer to himself as a "Dr." or, sometimes, "the Dr." And sometimes as "Duke." Also, Eric Hoffman not only has never worked as a "Professor," but he also dislikes schoolchildren, never graduated from college, and is an activist for home schooling. His insistence on the use of the title "Prof." is not only a legal misnomer, but a pathological cry for help.

Forgive us,
Eric Hoffman & Gary Rudoren

BEFORE YOU START READING / ABSORBING

We've debated amongst ourselves just what this book "wants" to be for you. We know that it's an invaluable manual for you and your life. Check. But the tough part is that we don't really know you. However, the important thing is that we think we do. First off, we believe that you are smart and intellectually curious. We're sure that you have a passion for self-knowledge and self-improvement. You care about others, including the elderly, children, and those that society has shunned. You're sensitive about your environment and you want to have nice things. You have "good" hair, probably. Or had. You're taller than you think you are. You celebrate tiny victories when you're not bitter. You rearrange the cookies in the box to make it look like you didn't take any. You're into porn, but don't tell people. You care what people think about you and use their opinion of you to determine your self-esteem.

Are we psychic or what? LOL.

Ultimately, we talked it over and decided that we weren't out of line with any of our assumptions and that you would be fine if we just gave you the information in an extraordinarily engaging manner. And with some funny pictures. Truly, we created this book for you. AND because we saw an opening. A "need," if you will. You see, generally, people fall into 3 categories when it comes to being funny:

1. People who are funny.
2. People who are not funny, but think they are.
3. People who are not funny, but would like to be.

We believe that you are one of these people. Research shows most likely you're #3, which makes this book perfect for you. There are lots of joke books out there, sure – those books repeat "jokes" from "comedians" and expect you to just steal material and further repeat the jokes as if they're your own. But we're not like those other books – we LIKE you, and we want to see you become funny on your own without having to make all that annoying memorization effort. Remember, while cribbing a line from Jerry Seinfeld about cell phones might get you into someone's pants at a party, it won't get you through a whole relationship. Being truly funny and popular WILL.

Alrighty, enough of our blather… Ready to start? Excited? Let the roller coaster ride begin!!!

SORRY, JUST A QUICK REMINDER
WHY THIS BOOK IS IMPORTANT TO YOU AND YOUR LIFE

> *"There are lots of comedy books out there.*
> *What will yours do for me? Me! Me! Me!"*
> —You

Look, we don't want to waste your time: if you find some other book that you think is somehow "better" than our woefully-underpriced-for-its-life-altering-value book, then by all means, call us up and we'll go out for coffee or something to discuss it — but for now, just look at these scientifically proven practical applications for **COMEDY BY THE NUMBERS.**©

When writing a screenplay:
1. Devise an interesting plot.
2. Develop characters that are organic to the context and serve the story.
3. Write a main part for an actor who is perceived as popular.
4. Remember that people love breasts.
5. Add bits from **Comedy By The Numbers.**©

When writing a stage play:
1. Select a moral imperative that you know will change your audiences' lives.
2. Conceive of characters that support your point of view, preferably British.
3. Inject an overwhelming metaphor.
4. If you want to make it funny, cast Nathan Lane.©
5. Add bits from **Comedy By The Numbers.**©

When writing a stand-up comedy act:
1. Try to be the audience's best friend (i.e. ask, "How are you doin' tonight?").
2. Search your background for irony (i.e., let's say you're Jewish (87% of stand-ups are), but your dad had a Hitler mustache).
3. Make observations about yourself and those around you that you believe are universal to the human condition.
4. If you are fat, talk about that.
5. Add bits from **Comedy By The Numbers.**©

When writing a situation comedy for television:
1. Place your characters in an environment that 36% of the viewers can relate to.
2. Don't be afraid of stereotypical characters or tired old plot devices.
3. Make all your characters caustic and hateful, except for the ones that are hot or ditzy.
4. Add bits from **Comedy By The Numbers.**© (avg. 50 per 22-minute episode.)

When at a party with people that you want to like you:
1. Hover on the edge of a conversation between two "cool" people as if you're part of their "posse."
2. Talk about how much money you have on you at any given moment.
3. Drop the names of celebrities who gave you an add on MySpace.
4. Add bits from **Comedy By The Numbers.**©

ADDED© BONUS! THIS EDITION ONLY!

As an Added© bonus and at no extra cost, you'll find several timely DATING TIPS scattered throughout this edition only! Let's face it, comedy is SEXY SEXY SEXY – and the systematic mastery of Pantomime and the Rule of 3s can certainly do you no harm in the lovin' department, if you catch our drift. So why not SPICE UP your marriage! Soon you'll be hearing, *"Mmm, baby, where did you learn that Mirror Routine? I'm sexually attracted to them. They make me wanna screw and screw and screw and screw screw screw screw screw screw screw screw! I want you now! With the Groucho glasses!"* Guaranteed! Or your FREE back!

MEET YOUR NEW FRIEND... "WEBSTER"

We're proud to introduce to you the comedic icon that will accompany you on your journey through **COMEDY BY THE NUMBERS.**© This original "everyman" will show up every once in a while throughout the book to add a graphic emphasis to the incredibly important words you're reading. In order to keep the book at a reasonable price, we made a brave decision: to create a unique graphic for which we would have to pay no royalties. Sure, photographs are "pretty," but if we've learned anything through the process of putting this book together, it's that the estates of dead comedy celebrities have unreal expectations when it comes to the value of photographs. So heeeeeereeee's Webster!

Illustrations by Sgt. Mike Falba

ABOUT THE ILLUSTRATOR

After losing the same leg twice in World War II, Sgt. Mike Falba was reassigned to the "light drawing" branch of the Military Manuals Dept. of the Interior. There he illustrated an array of howitzer technical manuals, hand-grenade schematics, syphilis-training booklets, and "What to do in case of mustard-gas attack" posters. After the war, Sgt. Falba found work with some of the most prestigious dictionaries in the country, illustrating such famous entries as *owl, heliotrope, mitten,* and *cog*. His work for this book is the last thing he completed before a triple heart attack felled him on Secretary's Day of this year. He is survived by his 18-year-old mute wife.

AND NOW, THE COMEDY BY THE NUMBERS©
NUMBERS!

YOU ARE SO CLOSE!

One last note, and if we're not saying it enough already we apologize, but please remember that this book is more than just a list of the best numbers comedy has to offer – it's SO MUCH MORE. Not only are there the "lists" (as promoted on the front and noted in the previous sentence), but also, at no extra charge, there are numerous examples of other data you can put into your "mental fun-o-dex"© including hilariously written sketches, humorous (yet scientific) diagrams, and comedy facts for you to throw out at parties, as well as pictures of some of the comedy shoulders from history that you'll be standing on every time you do a bit.

We realize in America anyone can just list things. That's the easy part – and it's protected by the Supreme Court. So, it was important to us that you don't think you're wasting your hard earned tip money. As you read along, we think you'll agree that COMEDY BY THE NUMBERS© is so much more than just a list! Now let's start with this almost alphabetical list.

1 ANIMALS DOING THINGS HUMANS DO
2 ANTI-AUTHORITARIANISM
3 ANTI-COMEDY
4 AUDIENCE PARTICIPATION
5 BARBS, RETORTS, COMEBACKS, SASSINESS, ZINGERS, & CAPPERS
6 BEING "ON"
7 BIG WORDS / MADE-UP WORDS
8 BLIND DATES
9 BOOGERS AND BONERS
10 BRAVADO / SNOBBERY
11 BREAKING THE 4TH WALL
12 BRITISH HUMOUR
13 CAN'T GET TO SLEEP
14 CATCHPHRASES
15 CELEBRITY ROAST
16 CLOWNS
17 COMIC STRIPS / GAG CARTOONS
18 CONDUCTING AN ORCHESTRA

19 CONTACT WITH SOMETHING THAT ISN'T DRY
20 CONTACT WITH SOMETHING THAT IS VERY HOT
21 CRAZY DANCES
22 "CRINGE" COMEDY
23 CROSS EYES
24 CURSING
25 DEATH / DYING
26 DEATH PORTRAYED AS AN ENTITY
27 DICK JOKE
28 DIFFICULTY WITH NUMBERS
29 DOCTORED PHOTOS / PRINT
30 DOUBLE ENTENDRE
31 DOUBLE-TALK / GIBBERISH
32 DRAMATIC ACTING STYLES
33 DRESS BLOWN OVER HEAD
34 DRUGGIE HUMOR
35 DUMMIES
36 DWARFS, MIDGETS, AND THE LIKE

37 EATING LIKE A PIG
38 ELABORATE DISGUISES
39 ENTRANCES / EXITS
40 EXCESSIVE VOMITING, BLEED-
ING, CRYING, LAUGHING,
SPITTING, BURPING, FARTING
41 EXCUSES
42 EXERCISING
43 EXTENDED DIRECTIONS AND /
OR EXPLANATIONS
44 FACIAL EXPRESSIONS
45 FAKE VOMIT, SHIT, URINE,
BLOOD, ETC.
46 FART NOISE
47 FOREIGNERS / ETHNICS
48 FUNNY COMPLAINT LETTERS
49 FUNNY EYEWEAR / FAKE
TEETH / PHONY WARTS
50 FUNNY NAMES
51 FUNNY PERSON PLAYING A
MUSICAL INSTRUMENT
52 FUNNY SLANG
53 GOSSIP
54 GROUP OF PEOPLE ENTER-
ING / EXITING AN AREA
THAT COULDN'T LOGICALLY
HOLD THEM
55 HIDING IN A COSTUME SHOP
56 HIPPIES
57 HUMOR FUNNY TO GAYS
58 ILLNESSES, AFFLICTIONS,
MALADIES
59 IMPOSSIBLE DISTANCES IN
SHORT TIME
60 IMPROVISATION / IMPROV /
IMPRO
61 INAPPROPRIATE BEHAVIOR
62 IRONY
63 JEWS & THEIR
IDIOSYNCRACIES
64 KIDS DOING THINGS
GROWN-UPS DO
65 KILLING A PERSON
66 KILLING A LOT OF PEOPLE
67 MAGIC
68 MAKING FUN OF SOMEONE
ELSE'S FLAWS
69 MEDICATIONS AND THEIR
SIDE EFFECTS
70 MENSTRUATION

71 MICKEY ROONEY
72 MICROPHONE BITS
73 MILITARY HI-JINX
74 MIMES / PANTOMIME
75 MIRROR ROUTINE
76 MISPRONUNCIATION
OF WORDS
77 MISSING TEETH / GAP TOOTH
78 MISSPELLING IMPORTANT
INFORMATION
79 MISTAKEN IDENTITY
80 MR. CLUMSY
81 MR. KNOW-IT-ALL
82 MOVIE SPOOFS
83 MUSICAL SPOOFS
84 NOT FUNNY AFTER REHAB
85 NON SEQUITURS
86 NOVELTY ITEMS
87 NOVELTY RECORDS
88 OBJECT WORK
89 OLD SCHOOL
90 ONE-MAN SHOW
91 ONE-UPSMANSHIP
92 ONE-DOWNSMANSHIP
93 OY VEY HUMOR
94 PAIN / REACTION TO PAIN
95 PATHOS a.k.a. CHAPLIN SYN
DROME a.k.a. THE THIRD MASK
96 PEE PEE JOKE
97 PEOPLE WHO SPEAK
OUR LANGUAGE
98 PEOPLE WHO DON'T SPEAK
OUR LANGUAGE
99 PERSONAL THEME SONG
100 PHYSICAL COMEDY / SHTICK
101 PIE IN THE FACE
102 PLAYING DRUNK
103 PLAYING MULTIPLE
CHARACTERS
104 POLITICAL JOKES
105 POO POO JOKE
106 PORTRAYING AN ANIMAL
107 PORTRAYING A
DIFFERENT SEX
108 PROP COMEDY
109 PUPPETS
110 RACIAL HUMOR
111 REFERENCING A
SITCOM CHARACTER

112 RELIGION
113 RETARDS / MENTALLY CHALLENGED
114 ROMANTIC COMEDY
115 RUBBER LEGS / LIMBS
116 SARCASM
117 SCARE COMEDY
118 SCHOOLYARD LAFFS & TAUNTS
119 SELF-DEPRECATION
120 SEX JOKE TELLING
121 SKETCHES / SKITS
122 SLAPPING
123 SLOW-MOTION FIGHTING
124 SOMEONE WHERE THEY DON'T WANT TO BE
125 SOMEONE WHERE THEY SHOULDN'T BE
126 SONG PARODY
127 SOUND EFFECTS
128 SOUND OF RECORD SCRATCHING TO A HALT
129 SPORTS HUMOR
130 SUBTLETY / UNDERSTATEMENT
131 SUPERHEROES / CARTOON CHARACTERS
132 SWITCHEROO
133 THE BEAT
134 "THE BLACKOUT"
135 THE CALLBACK
136 THE CLERGY
137 THE DELAYED REACTION
138 THE DEVIL / HELL
139 THE ELDERLY AND THEIR FOIBLES

140 THE FOIL
141 THE NICKNAME
142 THE PAUSE
143 THE TAKE
144 THE DOUBLE TAKE
145 THE TRIPLE TAKE
146 THE QUAD TAKE
147 THE UNLIMITED TAKE
148 THE SPIT TAKE
149 THE RULE OF 3s
150 THE RULE OF 4s
151 THE RULE OF 7s
152 THE "RUNNER"
153 THE SLOW BURN
154 THE SLOW FADE
155 TRANSPORTATION / VEHICLES
156 TRAVELING BITS / SCENARIO
157 TWO OR MORE PEOPLE TRYING TO GET THROUGH A DOOR AT THE SAME TIME
158 UGLY PEOPLE
159 UNDERWEAR
160 UNINTENTIONALLY FUNNY
161 VENTRILIQUISM
162 VERBAL ABUSE / SHOUTING
163 VOICE OVER SOMETHING THAT CAN'T TALK
164 VOODOO
165 WEDDINGS
166 WHITE TRASH
167 'WHO'S ON FIRST?'
168 WIGS
169 WOMEN (WOMYN variant)

THE SEQUEL, IF THERE IS ONE, WILL START WITH #170 – EXCITING, RIGHT?

We think you'll agree that this is an incredible list and that we obviously have put in a significant amount of time researching and compiling it.

"You're welcome!"

–Us

We know this page is blank.

#1 — ANIMALS DOING THINGS HUMANS DO

Impossible, you say? Chimps with grocery carts are funny! Cats using calculators while wearing accountant glasses are a riot! Animals are a lot smarter than we think they think we think, so don't coddle them. If getting a laugh means having your hamster put on a little thong, then don't think twice about whether or not said rodent is "embarrassed." Studies have shown that animals don't get embarrassed... and that's good for "us" comedy-wise.

CLASSIC EXAMPLE YOU'VE SEEN BEFORE

In every #114 (Romantic Comedy) film, you will find a cutaway shot of a cute pooch putting its paws over its eyes when its owner is getting kissed (and/or "something else") – as if dogs could blush! (See above embarrassment argument.) Include a cute pet in your life or your comedy career (sometimes they're the same), and you're guaranteed to get at least a smile.

EXTRA INSIGHT

While you might not get HUGE laughs with some of your "canine comedy," it might get you to second base if you're able to impress your date with anecdotes about how "Mr. Sprinkles makes decaf in the morning!" (Comedy Dating Tip!)

The Gold Standard: *Lancelot Link: Secret Chimp.*

Silver Medal: *Mr. Ed.*

HOW YOU CAN USE THIS IN YOUR REAL LIFE

Let's say you work in an office. That's not really the point, but the important thing is to have a dog or some other odd pet. Aside from the standard videos of unsuspecting men being hit in the nads, the "precocious pet" genre dominates *America's Funniest Home Videos.* (The authors recommend that getting on AFHV should be in your daily "goals" diary as one of your "things I need to accomplish" tasks – go for it! Think of all the people you can tell!) Maybe you have a dachshund named "Frankie" (funny already, huh?). One hilarious thing would be to dress him up in a little WWII Nazi uniform and have him sitting on a map of Poland with one of those mini hockey sticks, seemingly planning an invasion... do this at a party for your guests and you will provoke some hilariously nervous reactions! If you don't have access to doggie-sized Nazi uniforms, then perhaps you can post a video on your vlog (or on one of those websites that take videos of anyone doing anything) of your dog welding, or signing a car lease, or something else – and then stand back because you just might be the next web-star!

We encourage you to write down your thoughts as the book progresses. Note your goals and what part of what you just read inspired you. If you need more space to write, please buy another book.

_____

_____

_____

_____

_____

_____

---

comedy classics collector's stamps
CLIP 'EM AND COLLECT 'EM!

STOP!
GET USED TO THESE
SPECIAL LIMITED-EDITION, NO-HOLDS-BARRED, HILARITY-INCLUDED, COMEDY-CLASSIC STAMPS, BECAUSE THEY'LL BE COMING AT YOU THROUGHOUT THE BOOK

THE GORILLA SUIT
SERIES A
1

PETER SELLERS GLASSES
SERIES A
12

Cut out only if reverse side is not occupied with joke.

#2 — ANTI-AUTHORITARIANISM

So much of real comedy is about making the other guy look stupid, and we ALL laugh at our BOSS looking stupid! In order to get the most out of a good "Don't you hate 'The Man'?" bit, it's important to establish that you are not "The Man." This will get the audience on your side immediately (unless your audience is filled with "The Men," in which case, we recommend running offstage); you will automatically have them in the palm of your hand as you appeal to the popular common denominator of "hating." Remember: Just because someone is in a higher position at the office, makes more money than you, and takes on more responsibility, doesn't mean they're better than you. Comedy can be YOUR way of cutting them down to size.

WHERE YOU'VE SEEN THIS BEFORE

- TV's Sgt. Bilko, Phil Silvers, made a career out of making his superiors in the Army look like bumbling fools!
- TV's Sgt. O'Rourke, Forrest Tucker, made a career out of making his superiors at F-Troop look like bumbling fools!
- TV's Sgt. Schultz, John Banner, made a career out of being the dumb Nazi overseeing "Hogan" and his "Heroes" as they were constantly putting one over on him, his bemonocled superior, Col. Klink, and the crazily dangerous boobs at the Luftwaffe.

HISTORICAL FACT: There were unsubstantiated rumors during the Revolutionary War that the Hessians were overrun at Valley Forge by Washington's troops on Christmas Eve because they were busy planning a holiday revue mocking their superiors.

FURTHER ANALOGIES

Although we've cited several military examples, being anti-authority for comedy's sake can also apply to:

- Campers against Counselors (*Meatballs*)
- Caddies against Golfers (*Caddyshack*)
- Nerds against the Non-Nerds (*Revenge of the Nerds*)

#3 — ANTI-COMEDY

"What's this? The <u>absence</u> of comedy?! I paid good book money to be taught how to do <u>real</u> comedy! It isn't wise to cross me, Hoffman & Rudoren." That's you.

Here's us: *"But it's so easy to learn."*

Here's why: If your first instinct is to try <u>not</u> to be funny, then this bit guarantees you should go with your gut!

HOW TO USE THIS STEP BY STEP

1. Take a tried-and-true comedy staple.
2. Then accentuate, alter, prolong, comment on, or ignore one of its base elements.
3. What could be simply simpler?

EVERYDAY EXAMPLES FOR YOU TO USE

IGNORE: When asked "Who's on first?" – shrug and say "I don't understand baseball."

COMMENT ON: When hit in the face with a pie, say "I deserved it."

ALTER: Your reply to "knock, knock?" would be "no one's home." (Little kids love this one)

PROLONG: When dealing with a banana peel, either slip on it 65 consecutive times or beat up the peel.

(From our bold sister publication: ANTI-COMEDY BY THE NUMBERS©)

Even when you're not actually performing #3, it can save you untold embarrassment. **TO WIT:**

A FRIEND: "Gee, Bill, your jokes weren't that funny tonight."

BILL: "It was anti-comedy."

A FRIEND: "Hmmmmmmmmmmm… Oh! Great show!"

#4 — AUDIENCE PARTICIPATION

If you've ever been in the audience for any kind of stand-up or improv comedy routine – including hypnotism – then you know that audiences love nothing more than being asked to participate. Especially if they are asked to go on "stage." Most of the people in any given audience on any given night at any given comedy show hate their life. This is a scientific fact. But the chance to be on the "stage" gives them license to think that they then might be "discovered" by a big "Hollywood" person and/or get "laid" by their "date." Either way it's a win/win for you as the comedian in this scenario. As part of your arsenal of comedic ammunition, contrive some bits where you can deflect any negative feelings about you that the audience might have and transfer them to some rube from the audience.

A GREAT EXAMPLE

If you feel your stand-up comedy act is going poorly, try getting some vulnerable audience member on stage – a real fatty, for example – and interview them about their life, all the while pointing up the negative aspects.

"It figures that you're so fat – I don't think I've ever seen a SKINNY person working at the DMV! Am I right, everyone?!?" *(Said to the rest of the audience with a tone that conveys that of a confident plea for help.)*

They won't think that they're being made fun of because they're too busy thinking about how "cool" they now are!

This number combines extremely well with #68 (Making Fun of Someone Else's Flaws), #53 (Gossip), and sometimes a bit of #110 (Racial Humor).

FRIENDLY LITTLE REMINDER

When "improvising" on stage, remember that when you ask a drunken audience member for a "one-word suggestion" for your "improv" scene, it is perhaps wise not to anticipate this reply: "Politics!" Don't be upset. Without liquor, comedy would be nowhere.

#5 — BARBS, RETORTS, COMEBACKS, SASSINESS, ZINGERS, & CAPPERS

Or "Response Comedy," as some other lesser "books" call it. It sounds like a lot for one number, but we wanted to let you in on some of the words that professional comedians use when discussing comedy responses. It's good to have a list of these handy, because you never know when you will need to have a response to a heckler, your parents, or a first date. Instead of wasting time experiencing situations, sit alone in your room and think of situations that MIGHT happen and then create your own list of what you WOULD say if that DID happen. Also categorize your bits by noting different responses including but not limited to: Racial Taunts, Homophobic Asides, and Dismissive Hand Motions. Best if used sparingly, otherwise you run the risk of being looked upon as an asshole (see Dice Clay's career). The perfect companion number to #116 (Sarcasm) and/or #162 (Verbal Abuse).

HOW YOU CAN USE THIS IN YOUR REAL LIFE

Let's say you work in an office. It's the headquarters for a national company that makes products for a lady's "business." You've been working there for several years, but feel unappreciated. That's not really important for this scenario, but remember, good comedy comes from surface-level bitterness. Anyway, we bet that in that office is someone we all know – the "office bully." You've been sitting over in the corner not too far from the ladies' room, and every day when this bully goes to her restroom she knocks her big knuckles on your desk and says, "Wake up, sister!" (Even though you're actually a man and you're not asleep.) To make matters worse, she laughs her big horselaugh to herself, as bullies are wont to do. This can be very disconcerting, BUT now you can give her the ol' #5 by thinking of JUST THE RIGHT response! Here are a few suggestions for you... you!

- "Don't worry – I am so awake, it's scary! Boo."
- "Stop with your rudeness, or I'll tell everyone about your vaginal odor!"
- "What's good being awake if I have to listen to your stinky pie hole, whore?"*

*If your retort is in the form of a rhetorical question, it will stop anyone in their tracks as they have to mentally process through whether or not they should answer and, if so, what could "TOP" your use of 'whore!'

#6 — BEING "ON"

THIS NUMBER IS REALLY REALLY IMPORTANT!

IF you truly are looking to change your life and become more popular AND pursue a career in comedy, you need to be at your FUNNIEST at all times. We call it "Being ON."© "Never let anyone see the real you – just the funny you!"© (pending)

WHERE YOU'VE SEEN IT BEFORE

- Most frat parties
- Every time Robin Williams opens his mouth

#7 — BIG WORDS / MADE-UP WORDS

A common misconception is that you need to be smart and already know lots of words – not true! The great Sid Caesar started on the road to success (and pills) because of words he just made up.

TIP!

If you live alone at home (as most cool comedians do!), then try practicing making up words in response to telemarketing calls – those operators will love spending time trying to figure out what the H you're talking about!

SIMPLE COMEDY EXERCISE

Take a name of a professional sports team and a sexually transmitted disease – put it together and then tell people that you are applying for a job as a... "Yankee Genital Wart Salesman" – you won't be able to count the laughs!

IMPORTANT COMEDY-HISTORY REFERENCE

Once there was a bit called "Sniglets," created by funnyman Rich Hall. "Sniglets" were made up words to describe real things for which there weren't words, but for which there should be words... get it? One of our favorites (and please, Rich, don't sue us) is "ignisecond" (this is the amount of time that passes when you lock the car door and then your brain says to you, "The keys are still in the ignition!"). Here's one that we made up and submitted many years ago to Mr. Hall, but never heard back. We guess Rich didn't have a lot of time since he was already spending all that "Sniglet" money. The word is "cubalanche," and it explains what happens when you tip back a glass of soda to get the last bit of liquid and then the ice cubes come and hit you in the face. "Cubalanche" – it's very funny and now it's yours to use – free! Screw you, Rich Hall!

#8 — BLIND DATES

One of the oldest situational-comedy bits. Often requires the man and/or woman to be ugly and/or misshapen. Can lead to a #114 (Romantic Comedy) bit if both parties are actually attractive. Comedically, it works well with a #36 (Dwarf), a #16 (Clown), or even a #113 (Retard/Mentally Challenged).

LOCATION LOCATION LOCATION

Good (meaning funny) places for awkward blind dates include:

- Senate Sub-Committee on Drug Trafficking
- Dildo Emporium
- Herbalife Convention
- Active Volcano
- Seaside Village Dildo Emporium
- Spain
- AAA meeting
- Abortion-clinic reunion party
- Swim-up bar in the grotto of the Playboy Mansion
- Civil War re-enactment picnic and/or Civil War Dildo Emporium

WHERE YOU'VE SEEN THIS BEFORE

The movie *Blind Date,* starring Bruce Willis and Kim Basinger. Also the TV show *Blind Date,* hosted by Roger Lodge.

#9 — BOOGERS AND BONERS

Seriously, these are two words that can be dropped into any situation, including a joke or comedy sketch, and you'll have a higher mathematical probability of getting a chortle than with nearly any other words (okay, "Poopie" and "Doodyhead" compare favorably). We ALL have boogers and ALL you guys get BONERS, so why can't we just be open about it?!? Introduce the picking of a BOOGER – we mean a REAL pick, not just a nonchalant swipe at the edge of the nostril – to a dramatic scene and watch the uncomfortable laughs roll out.

PICTURE FOR EXAMPLE

- Priest picking his nose during a sermon.
- President with full finger up nose while signing a nuclear-test-ban treaty.
- Cancer doctor pulling a big greenie out and wiping it on a brain X-ray.
- Little kid picking a big booger and eating it during his mom's waxing.
- Any old woman saying the word "boner."

All of the above will get a reaction – laff-ranteed.©

HOW THESE WORDS CAN HELP YOU FIND YOUR DESTINY

We know that there are people who aren't even getting this far into reading about the magic of this number because they're so disgusted at the thought of "boogers" or "boners." Well, screw them. We suggest that you use these words as a test of friendship. When you meet people in school, or on MySpace, ask them what they think of the "B" words. If they show some disdain, then pick your nose, flick a booger at them, and then grab your man-crotch in protest! (If you're a woman, then you should still grab your crotch, because that would be really cool to see). These people could never be your real friends. Only hang out with people with whom you feel comfortable using these words. Even if it turns out that you only meet one person like that, a life of near loneliness is worth the price of the creative freedom you've established.

#10 — BRAVADO / SNOBBERY

Where to begin? Much like a good solid #2 (Anti-Authority) bit, the humor comes from creating a character with overwhelming bravado (or arrogance) and then making them look goddamn ridiculous. Often these snobs suffer from a serious clinical psychological disorder that makes them, in layman's terms, "assholes" (other synonyms include dicks, wads, dickwads, gaywads, gonads, jack-offs, jags, etc.). You don't have time to psychoanalyze these jerks, however; you just have to give them their much-needed comeuppance! Take the time to develop your arrogant character in such a way as to eliminate any possible chance of the audience liking him – it makes the situation, for example, where he gets puked on by a baby elephant, or shit on by a giraffe, or mistakenly sucked up a rhinoceros's vagina (these are all zoo or safari scenarios, by the way) all the more hilarious!

OUR FAVORITE SNOB
Jim Backus, TV's "Thurston Howell, the Third."

WHERE YOU'VE SEEN IT BEFORE
Famed for its "us vs. them" brand of gross-out humor, the acclaimed *Caddyshack* film is highlighted by the timely comeuppance of "Judge [the amazing Ted Knight] Smails"! Watch and learn how to take the stuffing out of a stuffed shirt. Also, in the famed near-documentary *Animal House,* the snotty frat boys (including a young Kevin Bacon, before he knew ANYONE) are handed their comedic asses by the boys of Delta House (including the now-dead John Belushi).

LITTLE-KNOWN FACT: The Germans did NOT bomb Pearl Harbor.

TIP!

So you say you want __16__ minutes of fame... then read this!

Real actors and comedians often struggle to find their
"hook"° — you know, the one thing they become known for
— forever! The characters below may be freely inter-
changed with other bits, props, costumes, etc. to create
comedy! Let us know how it goes!

- President / unusual height
- Nurse / faint "Hitler" mustache
- Policeman / odd hairline
- Gynecologist / inappropriate wig
- Priest / bawdy parrot on shoulder
- Teacher / fake scars
- Lawyer / soiled pants
- Plumber / "kick me" sign
- Rabbi / oversized yarmulke
- News anchor / one tooth
- Bank Teller / half beard
- Chef / peeling flesh
- Cowboy / visible tattoos
- Door to door salesman / three nipples
- Accountant / huge sweat stains
- Indian / eating disorder
- Waiter / fused nostrils
- IRS agent / "Boob Inspector" ball cap
- Dictator / noticeable smell
- General / flipper arms

AT NO ADDITIONAL CHARGE!
Now add a side-splitting catchphrase to the
mix! Friends will come running!

- "Ya can't blame me for this one!!"
- "I'm high! I'm finally high!"
- "My name is Steve!"

- "I feel sexual!"
- "That's what she said she said."
- "That's the last time I ever drink THAT!"

#11 — BREAKING THE "4TH WALL"

Although a stage often seems to only have one wall (and if you're doing stand-up, it's probably a brick wall), there actually is a scientifically proven "4th Wall" between any comedian and his or her audience. This wall is the invisible dividing point between those who are brave & daring patriots (the comedians – or you, if you'd like to think of yourself that way) and the lemming-like, need-starved audience. If you are looking to break out and be different, then go right ahead and smash through that wall and engage with the "little people" (we don't mean the #36 (Dwarves, Midgets, and the Like) crowd). People will be both surprised that you are chatting with them directly and excited for their interaction with a "celebrity" (that's you!).

LITTLE-KNOWN TRUE FACT: When George Burns first turned to the camera in his groundbreaking TV series to tell an anecdote about Gracie, the network recorded more than 5,000 calls and letters wondering why George Burns was talking to them directly.

ANOTHER EXAMPLE WORTH NOTING

The groundbreaking *It's Garry Shandling's Show,* which ran on cable television, often featured celebrities playing themselves. The cynical Garry would sometimes talk directly to members of the studio audience (breaking through the aforementioned "4th wall") about the absurdly funny situations he and/or his celebrity friends were in. Also, sometimes, at the live tapings, we heard Garry would hit on the hot audience members.

#12 — BRITISH HUMOUR

Invented and misspelled by the British.

> **COMEDY FACT!**
>
> Comedy chameleon Peter Sellers, who had a lifelong phobia of dying from a heart attack, died of a heart attack.

#13 — CAN'T GET TO SLEEP

Insomnia + noises accentuated to impossible levels = hilarity. Keep adding pillows until absurdity. **NOTE:** all sitcoms get around to this "cackler" eventually, so it's never too early to try to write the world's best "my-character-can't-get-to-sleep" bit!

CLASSIC EXAMPLE

Watch famed portly, alcoholic comedian W.C. Fields in his film *It's a Gift*. A ten-minute sequence throws everything in the book at W.C., who's trying to nap on the porch swing – a coconut falling down the stairs, a brat, loud neighbors, the wife, a traveling salesman, and finally the porch swing itself. Throughout, Fields is nothing less than put-upon and caustic – as he should be.

FREE SUGGESTIONS FOR SLEEPING ANNOYANCES

- Giggling gay ghosts
- Exponentially increasingly screaming cats
- Drive-by shooting below open bedroom window

#14 — CATCHPHRASES

The pot at the end of the "comedy-dollar rainbow"! You will have it made in the proverbial shade if you can devise just the right combination of words (and attitude) in a phrase that will sweep across the nation, not just sound cool to your friends. Ideally, you have access to a television show or nationally syndicated radio show with which to introduce your incredibly memorable phrase. Hopefully it's a show like a *Saturday NL, MADTelevison,* or one of the talkers like Dave, Jay, Conan, Craig, Jimmy, Jon, or Stephen's show. The money shot would really be to come up with a phrase that will become so popular that it's on T-shirts, mugs, greeting cards, tattoos, and used in English-language classes for immigrants. Always helpful if you can get teenagers to repeat it.

ALRIGHT, HERE ARE SOME FAMOUS CATCHPHRASES AND THE CHARACTERS THAT SAID THEM

- Bugs Bunny / "What's up, doc?"
- Jackie Gleason / "How sweet it is!", "And awaaay we go!"
- Abbott and Costello / "I'm a baaaad boy!"
- George Burns / "Say goodnight, Gracie."
- Gracie Allen / "Goodnight, Gracie."
- Chevy Chase / "I'm Chevy Chase and you're not."
- Richard Nixon / "I am not a crook" (include victory wave).
- Laurel & Hardy / "Here's another fine mess you've gotten me into."
- Steve Martin / "Excuuuse me!"
- Jerry Lewis / "Hey, lady!"
- Red Skelton / "Good night and God bless."
- Smothers Brothers / "Mom always did like you best."
- Pat O'Brien / "You're so fucking hot."
- Jeff Foxworthy / "You might be a redneck if…"
- The Goon Show / "He's fallen in da water!"
- Ed McMahon / "Heeeere's Johnny!"
- Jack Nicholson / "Heeeere's Johnny!"
- Jack Benny / "Well!"
- Flip Wilson / "Here come da judge."

comedy classics collector's stamps
CLIP 'EM AND COLLECT 'EM!

For best results, use COMEDY BY THE NUMBERS' new "Stamp-issors! – The scissors made specifically for clipping out stamps!" Now with 8 essential cutting minerals!

#15 — CELEBRITY ROAST

There is almost nothing funnier than making fun of someone in such a way that they think that you actually love them, when really you are jealous of everything they have and have had. This bit requires that celebrities not be too famous or memorable, but JUST MEMORABLE enough so that the viewer is embarrassed for both the roaster and the roastee.

EXAMPLE WE JUST MADE UP

A roaster we'd like to see: the Army drill sergeant. Imagine the following aimed at kindly old Bob Hope:

"Listen up, you faggot! You are one pussy hair away from honking me off permanently! Are you royalty? Queen Faggot! I want to see your bunk in a high state of dress-right-dress, sweet pea! While you're shining boots tonight, I'll be enjoyin' me a nice fur-burger! Why you lookin' at me? You wanna suck my dick or somethin'? Move out! Thank you, thank you. Seriously, we love ya, Hopey."

HOW YOU CAN USE THIS IN YOUR REAL LIFE

Let's say you work in an office. Maybe it's a storefront insurance office in a small, conservative Midwestern town and you've been there for 29 years. Let's also say there's a guy who has been there 42 years and is retiring. His name is Dave. If you want to earn your own little moment in the sun after having gone unnoticed in your desk over there in the corner for 19 of those 29 years, then ORGANIZE A GOODBYE-PARTY ROAST FOR DAVE! You'll have a blast compiling inside-joke references ("Nobody can misfile a claim like Dave!"), and also this would give you an opportunity under the "Roasting Rules" to issue some caustic jabs at the others on the dais (you don't really need a dais, by the way)... For example: *"Boy, Millie from Accounts Receivable sure dresses like a whore — but then again, she gets all the money, so maybe she SHOULD!"* (These bits will either make you popular or a pariah, but it's a risk to take!)

#16 — CLOWNS

Inappropriate clowns in non-clown occupations, e.g. clown/librarian, clown/priest, clown/abortionist, clown/private eye… all provide a rolling, consistent laugh. Also, clowns having nasty, dirty sex can provide a smirk, guffaw, and/or knee-slap. Many other numbers will work well with clowns including #8 (Blind Dates), #21 (Crazy Dances), and #40 (Excessive Vomiting, Bleeding, Crying, Laughing, Burping, and Farting)

HISTORICAL NOTE

Clowns have been around as far back as cavemen, when the cave tribes selected a member of each cave to distract the dinosaurs by doing silly physical actions. Early cave-clowns also started smearing their faces with berries for reasons still unknown, and throwing buckets of caveman shit at the dinosaurs. The archetypal clown character was created out of self-preservation, but has endured as a reminder to us all that at any moment we could be the next one to be eaten.

WHY CLOWNS "WORK" AT A CHILDREN'S PARTY

A person who chooses to become a clown already, clearly, has some psychological problems. Put this prone-to-madness character together with a bunch of sugar-junkie six-year-olds and you've got comedy.

We'll now lay out for you a party-scene scenario that goes from bad to worse to high-larious©! Don't just copy us, though! Try to create your own chain reaction of calamitous events at a child's party in order to provoke laughter.

Here goes somethin':

1. *Beautiful scenic day with the sounds of children playing and visuals of party decorations hung up in a suburban backyard. It's a party for little Billy.*
2. *Kids are playing out front on the lawn as the clown, Spongey, pulls up in his sputtering 1974 Dodge Dart that is seemingly filled with smoke on the inside.*
3. *Spongey gets out of the car, still holding an impossibly long bong, as smoke escapes from car.*
4. *Spongey, not noticing kids right away, takes one last drag on the bong before lifting his eyes and seeing the wide-eyed stares of amazement from the following:*

a. Cute freckled girl
b. Mother in apron
c. Father with regular pipe
d. Zaftig Mexican maid
e. Cute family dog

5. Sheepishly, Spongey throws bong into backseat, grabs a big bag of balloons and toys from the car. He smiles, dusts off his big tie, and closes the car door.

This scenario can then move forward with bits in several directions, including these scene suggestions:

- Spongey gets hit by bus while crossing street to party (could also be seen as tragic).
- Spongey gets the party going only to fall asleep in a chair next to a piñata. Kids gather to stare and poke a stick at him instead of piñata.
- Spongey is seen eating all the birthday cake (you know, because he's high).
- Birthday boy's mother notices Spongey's huge bulge in crotch and turns away in horror OR Birthday boy's grandmother notices Spongey's huge bulge in crotch and smiles suggestively.
- Spongey, while doing balloon-animal tricks, goes off on bitter rant about his own life being a big waste and how his ex-girlfriend is a big bitch and last night he caught her sucking off his best friend (make sure to get same reaction shots as per the list above).

As you can see, there are SO MANY places to go in comedy with a high, well-hung clown character, we should almost have a whole separate book. Essentially, you CANNOT LOSE with the addition of a clown in your comedy piece and/or life, so GO FOR IT!

CLOWN NAMES STILL AVAILABLE FOR GENERAL USE
Bricksy, ZoZo, Schnozzola, Kikey, Spanish Susie, Mr. Ballsformore, Cock-o, Cancerella, Mofo, Señor Muerto, Hair-oshima, Spoogie, The Wiggernator, Stone Phillips, Pantsy the One-Eyed Trouser Clown, Mr. Cornhole, Floppo the Dicknificent, Blazey the Arsonist Clown.

#17 — COMIC STRIPS / GAG CARTOONS

Print is still a viable career avenue for the humorous, and fun! With newspaper comic strips, imagine the joy of writing jokes for the same seven unchanging characters, six days a week, for TWENTY years! Now that's a gig! Animated holiday specials soon follow, e.g. "Happy Washington's Birthday, Optimistic Owl!"; "Carve The Turkey, Optimistic Owl!"; "It's Your Crucifixion, Optimistic Owl!"

Look to your right for comics in action!

#18 — CONDUCTING AN ORCHESTRA

This "site-specific" comedic bit does in fact require some big bucks for the aforementioned orchestra. However, if you're writing a big-budget comedy and can somehow get your characters into the middle of a big classical concert venue (organically, of course), then you MUST include a put-upon, ex-Eastern-bloc conductor character!

SUGGESTED BITS
- Being distracted by the bosom of a woman in the audience
- Being drunk and waving your baton like a drunk person
- Speeding up the tempo as you try to swat a fly
- Not knowing how to conduct because you've been forced by drug dealers to conduct the symphony or your family will die (sometimes not funny)

Oh, also you must have a tuxedo.

WHERE YOU'VE SEEN THIS
Foul Play with Chevy "Fletch" Chase and Goldie "Have you seen my sweet ass?" Hawn – with Dudley Moore (who had a club foot).

GAG CARTOONS

For a perspective on the #17, we turn the book over to rascally cartoonist Chic Tongue. Chic's work has appeared in such mags as *Ribald*, *Rapscallion*, and *Barracuda*. He's the author of *1000 Jokes or Gags*, *Kissing With Tongue*, and *Tongue on Rye*. Chic (pronounced "chick") is the school they tore down to <u>build</u> the "old school." Listen (to yourself reading this) and learn!

"Here's how I keep my cartoons relevant: I don't! Nuts to relevant! A funny basic gag is one of the few constants in the universe. (I think Newton said that.) The basic funny idea behind the concepts of booze-hounds, mothers-in-law, battle-axe wives, and henpecked husbands transcends all time and culture. See below — the references in the punch lines are changed, but the joke is still the same, and it's still funny. (Notice that some joker at Rapscallion inked in sideburns on the husband in the 1969 version to make him more "hep." I had to white 'em out when I re-used the art next time. I remember I was pretty steamed about that extra work.)"   —CHIC

From *Stars & Stripes*, 1944

"Here comes the Gestapo – I mean -- your mother."

From *Rapscallion* Magazine, 1968

"Here comes the Viet Cong -- I mean -- your mother."

From *Rogue* Magazine, 1980

"Here comes the Ayatollah -- I mean -- your mother."

From *Barracuda* Magazine, 1998

"HERE COMES THE MENENDEZ BROTHERS -- I MEAN -- YOUR MOTHER."

#19 — CONTACT WITH SOMETHING THAT ISN'T DRY

One of the earliest examples of film comedy, this subversive shtick bit started in the silent-film era and included a famous image of Charlie Chaplin's pants as he walks away from a park bench. Charlie, not realizing that he had sat on a freshly painted bench, reaches around, and taps his fingers against the paint stain on his rear end. He then brings the finger up to his nose to smell it, as if he had inadvertently moved his bowels while on the bench and soiled himself. Convinced that he had in fact NOT done that, he twirls his cane and continues walking off into the sunset while we all laugh at what MIGHT have been!

Statistically, 99% of comedic sketches incorporating this bit specifically include someone mistakenly moving a large "wet paint" sign.

IMPORTANT TIP

The more dressed up the "victim" the funnier, i.e. the Pope, a virgin debutante, wandering minstrel, secretary general of the U.N.

WHERE YOU'VE SEEN THIS BEFORE

Almost every episode of TV's *Laugh-In* featured a freshly painted bench bit – often with Ruth Buzzi. And, on a related note, this groundbreaking wackfest of a show featured Goldie "Have you seen my sweet ass?" Hawn. (*Note: The mention of Goldie Hawn's ass in consecutive numbers is purely unintentional, but true.*)

WRITES ITSELF!

WRITES ITSELF!

The #19 is one of those special numbers that is so easy it "writes itself." Honest, you don't have to do a thing! Other "Writes Itselfs" to keep an eye out for: #27, #96, #105, #136, #159, and #163.

#20 — CONTACT WITH SOMETHING THAT IS VERY HOT

This action is of course very funny on its face, because it involves some injury (to other people) – however, it is the reaction to this bit that holds all the laughs!

WRITE THIS DOWN:

When your character inadvertently is in contact with something hot (e.g., spicy food, flame thrower, anthrax), an extended search for something cool or wet is best, perhaps ending with a dunking into an exotic-fish tank or jumping into a swamp in a prom dress. You can't OVERreact too much when it comes to this physically challenging number!

WHO'S THE KING

There've been a lot of great heat-reactors in the history of comedy; according to Carl Reiner (who knows from pain), Sid Caesar's responses were among the very best in the biz. But most comedians (Caesar included) say Laurel and Hardy top this list. Stan and Ollie also excelled in these reactions: ladder in the eye; stepping on upturned nails; giant saw blade falls on head; electrocution.

RELATED OLD JOKE THAT SHOULD BE RETIRED (BUT THAT THE KIDS LOVE)

What did the first man to walk on the sun say?
"Ouch, my feet! This is hot! Fuck, Cockfucker, Cunt!"

#21 — CRAZY DANCES

There are institutionalized crazy dances such as "The Macarena," "The Hustle," and "The Hora" that will always make us laugh, especially if performed by non-dance types (i.e. paraplegics or prison matrons). The challenge to breathing new life into this bit for comedic effect is to use both your imagination and your feet to create a dance that will make you the most popular person at any bar mitzvah.

HOW YOU CAN USE THIS IN YOUR REAL LIFE

Let's say you work in an office. And every year at the annual office Chrismukkahzaa Party, one of the employees announces that he/she is going to do a dance, "Just like Elaine did on *Seinfeld*!" and then dances awkwardly to the amusement of all, thinking that he/she is being original. Right. Well, next year it's your turn! Take your time and dedicate yourself to creating an interpretative dance showcasing the history of your office. Include hilarious imitations of your bosses and the service people, accentuating their physical flaws. Then at next year's office bash — or even a spring outing at the local bowl-o-rama — you spring it on everyone! You will rock! Also, if you're a fat guy, it's good for a laugh if you can tie up your T-shirt so it rests on top of your big stomach. People will love you for your creativity in the face of your obesity. Let us know how it goes!

BEWARE: Get a #113 (Retard/Mentally Challenged) to do this and you run the risk of bumming out your audience.

#22 — "CRINGE" COMEDY

The "cringer" in this number is the audience, who typically aren't used to seeing/hearing this brand of "body fluids" humor. Done correctly, it can define a generation.

HALL OF FAME

>   2000s: Howard Stern show
>   1990s: Sperm hair gel in *There's Something About Mary*
>   1980s: *Caddyshack 2*
>   1970s: Divine eating dog shit in *Pink Flamingos*
>   1960s: Long hair
>   1950s: The Kinsey Report

1940s: Accidentally kissing an "ugly girl"
1930s: Being "dry"
1920s: Erich Von Stroheim movies
1910s: Tripping over your own feet
1900s: Geek eats bat head in circus sideshow

#23 — CROSS-EYES

Deadliest when conjoined with a #94 (Pain/Reaction to Pain). Silent-film king Ben Turpin had his crossed eyes insured against uncrossing with Lloyd's of London. Lloyd's paid big when the painful wound from a nail Turpin had stepped on, which had caused the eye crossing in the first place, mysteriously healed with medical attention. Turpin's career ended in shit-pile ruins. The irrefutable lesson? If it makes you funny, don't fix it.

HOW THIS CAN HELP YOU BE POPULAR

It's no secret that people love to watch other people with deformaties – especially if they can manipulate their bodies in odd ways. They become the hit of any party they go to (although they often go home from that party alone). You know the ones we're talking about – the girl who can pick up a beer bottle with her abnormally long tongue; the boy so skinny he can put his arms around his back and then touch them in the front; the fat guy who can hide a desk calculator in the folds of his stomach; etc.

If you're not incredibly funny naturally, this is perfect for you! Learn to cross your eyes as a reaction to any situation, and just like the popular freaks noted above, you'll be the "Ben Turpin" of your social scene!

#24 — CURSING

No serious dissertation on cursing could ignore George Carlin and his famous fight against the FCC regarding his desire to use his potty mouth. His "Seven Dirty Words" routine is famous for its introduction of "Shit, Piss, Fuck, Cunt, Cocksucker, Motherfucker, and Tits" into the everyday lexicon. Thank you, George.

There are comedy snobs who believe that cursing is the lowest common denominator of humor and should be avoided at all costs. We respectfully disagree. As a matter of fact, we think that the introduction of a curse word into the middle of a word or phrase can not only achieve a welcome uncomfortable laugh, but may also express the seriousness of a situation – thereby accomplishing two things. For example:

An airplane pilot on his radio – we hear:

> "Roger, Ro-fuckin-ger, we need a big motherfucking shitload of money for these Islamo-stinkyasscist terrorists! Can you hear me? We've been hi-fucking-jacked!"

Now this is obviously a serious situation, made even more serious (and hilarious) by the creative cursing! Okay, a happy example:

In a restaurant, at a candlelit table – we hear:

> "I can't in a shitmillion years believe how happy you make me. Not in my wild-cocksucking-est dreams could I have imagined the J-O-pissingmyself-Y that I feel today! Yes, I'll fucking marry you! Yes!"

We almost want to cry.

TO SHOW YOU HOW UP-TO-DATE WE ARE

Please note the innovative use of "Kelly Clarkson" as a curse word in the semen-al film comedy, *The 40-year Old Virgin*. The use of anyone from *American Idol* as a curse is possible.

OTHER GOOD CURSE WORDS

Cockfuck, dicklicker, snatchfaggot, pooty, Eddie, shitmama, asswhore, spermagnet, titwhisperer, Spinoza, taintmaster, spermtard, cuntard – actually almost anything that ends in "tard."

#25 — DEATH / DYING

The groundbreaking *Weekend at Bernie's* series of films was recently embalmed in the Library of Congress's Movie Comedy Collection. ("Embalmed"... get it?) This movie should be studied for its ability to wring laughter from a series of situations that included the main character, who was dead. Normally those who are dead are mourned; in this case, Bernie was dragged around a beach.

KNOW YOUR COMEDY LINGO

"Death" or "Dying" also can mean a tough-luck situation in comedy; it can be a slang term used by stand-up comics after leaving an audience who they claim didn't "get" his/her jokes. A comedian might say "I died out there" with regard to their show. This is an over-exaggeration by the comedian in an attempt to win sympathy.

OTHER COMEDY LINGO FOR "DYING"
- "That audience can suck my fucking dick!"
- "Hmph. Guess I wasn't <u>dirty</u> enough for 'em."
- "Come on, I was funny out there. Right? That was funny..."
- "Faggots!"
- "<u>Wow</u>."
- "Whew!"
- "No – it was <u>my</u> fault."

WHERE YOU'VE SEEN DEATH BEFORE... AND LAUGHED!
- *Defending Your Life*
- *Heaven Can Wait*
- *Here Comes Mr. Jordan*
- *Monty Python's Meaning of Life*
- *Love and Death*
- *Death Race 2000*
- *Interiors*

> **COMEDY FACT!**
>
> Comedy legends Abbott & Costello, although funny, funny men, hated each other and are now dead.

#26 — DEATH PORTRAYED AS AN ENTITY

We all live in fear. At least the both of us do. And one of the only things that helps us get up in the morning is the thought that when the day comes that we are chosen to merge with the eternal, there standing on the other side of the river Styx is the Grim Reaper wearing Groucho glasses and mustache. Wouldn't that be hilarious! Sorry for the psychological confession there, but the point is, don't miss an opportunity to stick it to "The Man" (see #2). Fuck you, Death, we say!

In this case, "The Man" is the Reaper himself, so why not embarrass him by having him appear in your hit comedy film and/or play as:

- An ice-cream salesman
- Bumbling civil servant
- An adorable doggie
- Crotchety librarian
- Smarmy bellboy

You might even be able to bring to it what some call "levels," and all the hoi polloi will think that by portraying Death as, for example, an inept bicycle-repair salesman, you're making some big point about the "journey we're all on" or some other such crap. Screw that; it would just be funny watching the GR try to change a flat tire!

CAUTION: This device has been used so much by Woody Allen, there are rumors he's starting to repeat himself.

#27 — DICK JOKE

Second only to #159 (Poo Poo Joke) as your top common-denominator go-to joke. There are two schools of thought: One says that the key is to use <u>your</u> dick and/or its various nicknames: cock, tuber, prick, joystick, polish sausage, wang, throat-tickler, mushroom-manny, skin-cicle, frankfurter, heat-seeking missle, rock-throbster. You can show how comfortable you are in your manhood by assigning a personality to your penis.

HISTORICAL NOTE: Former "Perfect Stranger" Mark-Linn Baker once played the voice of Griffin Dunne's penis in a movie. We would tell you which one, but quite frankly everyone involved is still embarrassed.

The other school of thought says you'll get laughs by just telling someone else that they've got a small dick.

Either way, the word "dick" is a funny word and can be thrown in as a noun, verb, adjective, and "dangling" modifier (get it?).

KEEPIN' IT REAL

If sexual discrimination truly exists, it is to be found here in the realm of gags about reproductive organs. For some baffling reason, the penis has always been a laugh magnet; while the ladies' "bizness" is, in the comedy world, generally viewed as... well, let's just say I wouldn't "close" with it.

comedy classics collector's stamps
CLIP 'EM AND COLLECT 'EM!

PANTOMIME PINKY	THE IRRITATING FLY	THE PANTOMIME HAT
SERIES A 10	SERIES A 18	SERIES A 6

For best results, stamp should be adhered to top of other very expensive rare stamp.

#28 — DIFFICULTY WITH NUMBERS

Once again, you don't have to be smart or stupid to master this bit... just be able to count!

TRIED-AND-TRUE BIT

One character is trying to count a lot of money; the laughs erupt when the other character, usually unknowingly, mentions a series of statements/questions that include other numbering systems, thus causing the first person to... lose count!

SAMPLE SCENE (ABSOLUTELY USEABLE BY YOU, JUST BECAUSE YOU BOUGHT THIS BOOK!)

[*Two men are standing at a hospital-ward pharmacy counter. One is a male nurse (Bob). The other one is dressed in a leisure suit and has a map (Stu). Bob has a pile of pills in front of him.*]

> **BOB**
> Okay Stu, don't bother me, because I have to make sure that all the AIDS pills are here so no one on the ward floor overdoses. *(counting out loud)* 1, 2, 3, 4...

> **STU**
> Hey Bob, I've got to go pick up my pants at the cleaners over on 18th street.

BOB

18, 19, 20...

STU

Should I take the 85 bus?

BOB

85,86,87,88...

STU

Or just pick up a cab in the Village
at 4th Avenue?

BOB

4th, 5th, 6th...

STU

You know what, forget that, I'm just
going to walk the 102 blocks! (*Exits.*)

BOB

102, 103, 104. Done... Well, I've got
all the pills for the homosexuals and
drug users, and I'm sure the AIDS
crisis will be over in no time!
(*Looks down at the 17 pills in his
hand (he thought he had 104, remember?) and exclaims "YOW-ZA" and does
a #144 (The Double Take).*)

THE END

COMEDY FACT!

Fatty Arbuckle, the first "fat" comedian, was
accused of rape and sodomy. Although acquit-
ted, his career ended in ruin.

#29 — DOCTORED PHOTOS / PRINT

Visual comedy at its easiest; the ability to cut and paste can be the answer to any #, with a caution to add #62 (Irony). For example: punch up your visuals with an old person's head on a whore's body – or vice versa!

WARNING!

This number is, no doubt, the bit most likely to be reinvented in this new age of technology. "Photoshop" is to the world of comedy as cheese was to the burger – it makes it taste so much better. If you're reading this and you're not "wired" (have a computer), then go out to Best Buy or some other "computer" store and get one now. Don't forget to mention this book (it won't get you a discount, but it will help spread the word about the book). Once you're able to take digital photos and then manipulate them to create hilariously embarrassing photos, phony police reports, and incriminating background information – then all you need to do is "e-mail" everyone you can and ask them to "spread the word." Word of your wacky sense of humor will spread throughout cyber-land and you could get a "reputation." Case in point is those guys that did that crazy hilarious photo that was supposedly taken from the observatory at the top of the World Trade Center with the plane right behind the smiling doofus. Those guys were funny.

#30 — DOUBLE ENTENDRE

For sophisticates only; as Mr. David Niven liked to say, "That kind of humor is hard on me, but I'll give it a crack". *Hard on* is also a name for an erect penis, and *crack* can alternately refer to one's anus and/or a vagina. Thus you can see how funny it is for a debonair fellow such as David Niven to be somehow alluding to fucking. Basically, you're saying something to someone about having sex with them, without saying that you want to have sex with them. This brand of "sex comedy" is also the most accessible to bachelors (Comedy Dating Tip!). Liven up a #114 (Romantic Comedy) with a few of these.

HERE ARE SOME FUNNY FOLKS WHO CAN "DO" THIS BIT:

Benny Hill, Bill Clinton, Sean Connery, Roger Moore – but, curiously, never Hugh Hefner.

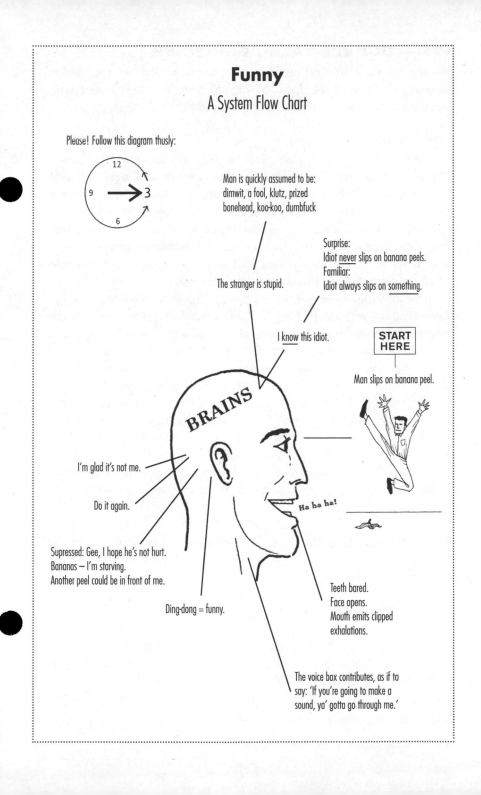

Funny
A System Flow Chart

Please! Follow this diagram thusly:

Man is quickly assumed to be: dimwit, a fool, klutz, prized bonehead, koo-koo, dumbfuck

Surprise:
Idiot <u>never</u> slips on banana peels.
Familiar:
Idiot always slips on <u>something</u>.

The stranger is stupid.

I <u>know</u> this idiot.

START HERE

Man slips on banana peel.

BRAINS

I'm glad it's not me.

Do it again.

Ha ha ha!

Supressed: Gee, I hope he's not hurt.
Bananas — I'm starving.
Another peel could be in front of me.

Ding-dong = funny.

Teeth bared.
Face opens.
Mouth emits clipped exhalations.

The voice box contributes, as if to say: 'If you're going to make a sound, ya' gotta go through me.'

#31 — DOUBLE-TALK / GIBBERISH

The Czech call it "the art of making nonsense sound like real words for comedic effect." Happily, they're in complete agreement with everyone else in the world who understands the concept.

HOW TO DO IT

Let's say you want to "double-talk" in German (example) or speak "German gibberish." First of all, for this number you don't actually need to <u>know</u> German, so breathe easy. Indeed, that's part of the fun fun fun of it all – the audience loves the fact that you don't know what the fuck you're saying! But you <u>will</u> have to pinpoint the recurring rhythms, sounds, and catchphrases of the German language. This is what is known as "profiling," and it's the only time you'll ever be able to use it without fear of being socially scorned.

Now just run all of these sounds, etc. together like you've been "spreching" all your life. <u>Example:</u> "Machen zi leiber der hausfrausen die eisen-steinen machen!" This could mean anything! And probably does!

There, that wasn't so "hardenzi" was it? *Now here's the comedy key to #31:* at the end of every sentence, add an English word or phrase so the audience is let in on what you're talking about (the joke you're making). <u>Example:</u> "Machen zi leiber der hausfrausen die eisen-steinen machen – I <u>hate</u> tofu!" Gales of laughter follow! Here's the Laff-rhythm© you should be boppin' to: "Gibberish gibberish gibberish gibberish gibberish – English-language joke!"

"Baby talk" is a great example of gibberish, and the same Laff-rhythm© applies: "Goo goo, ga ga, doody-doody-doody – where's all the tits!"

ALSO RECOMMENDED! Go to your local maternity ward and ask to "sit in with the newborns" – it should be no problem. And bring a tape recorder, you perfectionist you.

FUN FACTS ABOUT THIS NUMBER

In the 1940s, #31 was best set up with: "You know how them Germans talk – it's all 'machen zi' this and 'heil-en zi' that."

Crocodile Dundee was thought to be a brilliant gibberish comedian until it was discovered he was just a foreigner.

DOUBLE-TALK/GIBBERISH — WHO YOU SHOULD STUDY (FOR REALS)

- Sid Caesar (so good he's almost foreign)
- Anyone who's performed with Sid Caesar
- Danny Kaye
- Most vaudeville comedians
- Sports Nuts (Am I right, ladies?)
- Women (Who's with me?)

#32 — DRAMATIC-ACTING STYLES IN COMEDY

On its surface, this might seem like a clear #3 (Anti-Comedy), but no! If you want to be a REAL comedian, then it's important that you discover your "dark side."© In the comedy world, no one is respected more than those who have CHOSEN to be unfunny. In the non-comedy world, while we stand by our premise that girls dig a funster, we also know that chicks love a guy who can get in touch with his serious side. Those guys get BJs like you wouldn't believe.

PRACTICE, PRACTICE, PRACTICE

You don't need to work in an office for this one. Try being dramatic at home with your folks (if you're still lucky enough to be living at home with them):

- Turn over a plate of food your mom just made and weep into your hands.
- Throw a condensed version of large-print *Reader's Digest*s at the TV and run to the basement screaming.
- Shit yourself during a family intervention.

SIDE NOTE: When a comedian performs with a "serious" style in a comedy show, it can be very funny indeed. However, that same style in a serious show comes across as hokey and self-indulgent. Comedians who want to prove they can do "straight" material are forewarned: "remember the bit" (i.e. remember what got you where you are/what made you popular). Few people have much patience for comedians who refuse to do a comedy role ("refuseniks"). Person probably needs a good #72 (Mirror Routine).

- Robin Williams – *Good Will Hunting*
- Robin Williams – *Patch Adams*
- Robin Williams – *One Hour Photo*
- Robin Williams – *Dead Poet's Society*

#33 — DRESS BLOWN OVER HEAD

The giggles for this number are as unpredictable as fashion itself. Works best with a high-society dame wearing "Porn Star" underwear.

OTHER "CLOTHING MEETS NATURE" BITS
- Wearing a Vera Wang original / golf-ball hail
- Putting on a tie clip / volcanic eruption
- Shining up a new derby / Katrina
- Stepping out of the store with a new toupee / pelican falls in love with it

#34 — DRUGGIE HUMOR

Ironically, invented before drugs. You should always give the impression that you have done lots of drugs. Don't believe all the public-service BS; people will think you're cool if you've "toked," "snorted," or "booted junk!" When you're on stage doing your "comedy," you can use "your drug habit" as an excuse if a joke bombs – for example, you can say, "Wow, I don't even know what I just said – I guess I shouldn't have shoved an eight ball of crank up my ass when I wrote that one." THEN you'll get the outrageous laugh you were looking for in the first place!

HOW YOU CAN USE THIS IN YOUR REAL LIFE

Let's say you work in an office. Most offices have strict zero-tolerance drug policies. Let's say that it's "that time of year" again, when the suits are going to test everyone's urine for traces of illegal drugs. This is a perfect scenario for you to pull the following hilarious prank:

1. Find a junkie on the street
2. Secure some of his or her urine
3. Somehow substitute their junkie pee for the urine of one of the people you hate in the office.
4. The trick is finding JUST THE RIGHT TIME to tell everyone about the "big joke" before the police show up!
   No one will be able to top this, we promise!

HISTORICAL FACT

The catchphrase "What are you, high?" is the only joke simultaneously invented on both coasts.

WHERE YOU'VE SEEN DRUGGIE HUMOR

- Cheech & Chong's *Up In Smoke*
- *Richard Pryor Live on the Sunset Strip*
- The offices of *Saturday Night Live*

THE TRUTH, DUDE, THE TRUTH

Watching actors in a film or TV show pretend to get high by smoking dummy-weed WILL make you want to get high yourself! Luckily, drugs = humor.

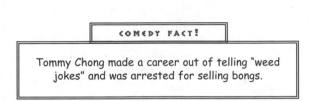

COMEDY FACT!

Tommy Chong made a career out of telling "weed jokes" and was arrested for selling bongs.

#35 — DUMMIES

HISTORICAL FACT TO START WITH

This comedic standard-bearer was invented during the Renaissance by the renowned scientist Copernicus, who threw a full-size fabric likeness of himself over a tower in a piazza in Florence on a bet from a nobleman. The "phony" Copernicus first brought gasps and then guffaws (in Italian) to the throngs below. Later, it was the real Copernicus who was hung for his heretic theories. But the "dummy" has endured and become a nearly guaranteed bit of business that ALWAYS takes the audience by surprise!

MORE HISTORY

During the Great Depression, the use of the "Okie Dummy" in early silent-film comedies turned the nation's tears... to laughter!

TO THE DUMMY-SHOPPER

Hello, dummy-shopper! Here's a friendly word of advice for you: When perusing the dummy-wears of your local prop shop, be sure to make a selection that follows the strict rules of dummydom. Make sure you get the dummy that has the limbs that flail and bend in impossible directions; the one that obviously weighs far less than an actual human body. You know, the one that's like a big sack made of human flesh without any bones or guts or muscle mass inside of it. This is the dummy audiences recognize and trust. They know they're in competent hands when ol' crazy legs shows up. Your reward is a laugh, dear student. And nothing more.

COMEDY FACT!

TV pioneer Ernie Kovacs' first wife kidnapped their children after an ugly divorce. Although he eventually located them, he later died in a car crash.

#36 — DWARFS, MIDGETS, AND THE LIKE

Like the Bible, we won't shy away from the truth. At the risk of being put in "politically incorrect jail"©, let's face it – we ALL laugh at people that don't look like us. If this book were to be primarily promoted in the Midget/Dwarf community, there is no doubt we would have referred to the "Tall" or "Fat" for this section. But government studies have shown that there aren't actual separate bookstores for those people, and even if there were, they just don't buy a lot of comedy books. Thus, we are appealing to a "Taller" audience! This bit is a true test of your ability to find the "hilarity in the humanity"©!

WARNING! It seems like a no-brainer to just toss a midget into any scene and it will be funny, but **THAT'S WRONG!** That's for amateurs! If you want to be a serious comedy professional, then don't overlook dwarf and midget bits in their proper form. (We'll call them Little People from now on because those people like to be called that.)

SOPHISTICATED LITTLE PEOPLE BITS

- Place important objects too high on a shelf for them to reach. You'll get laughs out of their attempts to jump and/or build a tower out of couch cushions. **SUGGESTION:** Make it something really important like an insulin syringe.
- Put them in scenes with abnormally tall people, but give them the same goal; i.e. a little person at a job interview is in the waiting room sitting next to another applicant… Manute Bol! (Very tall African basketball failure.)

IF YOU WANT TO SOUND REALLY SMART…

Remember the name Billy Barty. If you need to throw a reference to a famous midget into a joke, plug in "Billy Barty." He was an actual actor and midget (little person) – and great at both! You will always get a chuckle from the hi-brows in the crowd (or at least Dennis Miller) with this reference.

Example of "smart joke with Billy Barty reference" (stand-up comedy classification):

> *"So, I dated this girl for awhile and it was going great – until we had sex. It was all downhill from there because afterwards she told me that my dick wasn't as big as BILLY BARTY'S DICK."*

WE'RE SORRY TO INTERRUPT THE LIST, BUT WE THOUGHT NOW WAS A GOOD TIME TO BRING UP A QUESTION WE GET ASKED ALL THE TIME... WHO IS THE GREATEST COMEDY CHARACTER EVER?

WELL, OUR VOTE GOES TO... INSPECTOR CLOUSEAU

In five blockbuster comedies (and one posthumous outing), Peter Sellers and Blake Edwards presented what is arguably the greatest comedic character ever created. Few characters have enjoyed such amazing success, and few characters have used so many comedy numbers so brilliantly, including: clumsiness, anger faces, physical comedy, pain reactions, slow-motion fighting, crazy foreign accents, romantic comedy – just to name a few. Director Edwards and Sellers shared a love for the geniuses of slapstick and visual humor: Laurel & Hardy, Keaton, Lloyd, Tati. They also collaborated on a kind of unofficial Clouseau film, *The Party*.

FOR THE COMEDY NERD WITHIN YOU, MEMORIZE THE FOLLOWING: THE FIRST-EVER ANALYSIS OF THE PANTHER OEUVRE

> *The Pink Panther* (1964) – Clouseau is the comic relief of the film. There's not a lot of screen time, but what there is was enough to spawn a golden franchise. We suggest starting with...

A Shot In The Dark (1964) – Clouseau is the main character. Also introduced: Burt Kwouk as his manservant Cato, who's been instructed to attack him whenever possible, just to keep him on his toes; and the genius Herbert Lom as Clouseau's boss, Chief Inspector Dreyfus, who is driven realistically insane. Chicks dig this one the most (Comedy Dating Tip!).

Inspector Clouseau (1968) – Alan Arkin (Clouseau) and Bud Yorkin (director) take over for a weird entry in the series. For collectors only.

The Return of the Pink Panther (1975) – Their careers in a slump, Sellers and Edwards return in high form. Clouseau's absurd disguises come into their own.

The Pink Panther Strikes Again (1976) – Our personal favorite, but don't start with this one – like any good series, it's better to know how the characters got to this point. In many scenes, Edwards simultaneously juggles several hilarious bits.

The Revenge of the Pink Panther (1978) – Everyone's a little off; still, even off, Sellers is masterful. The great Robert Loggia also stars.

The Trail of the Pink Panther (1982) – Even Sellers's death couldn't stop Edwards from releasing a new Clouseau flick. Includes unused footage of Sellers from previous films, which is always good. Among the living, only Lom entertains; like seeing a Hardy movie without Laurel.

The Curse of the Pink Panther (1983) – And so begins the line of thinking that Clouseau is like Bond – the franchise can survive no matter who stars (Ted Wasssss). The Bond people were wrong on many levels – but the Panther people were just stupid. Forget it. (Except for Lom.)

Son of the Pink Panther (1993) – Roberto Benigni as Clouseau's illegitimate son. Lom's last. A real stinker. (Except for Lom.)

The Pink Panther (2006) – Without Herbert Lom, Peter Sellers or Blake Edwards, who the fuck gives a fucking shit.

#37 — EATING LIKE A PIG

Gross-out humor always works with the cool crowd! Especially funny if character is clinically obese; also borders on sad.

WHERE YOU'VE SEEN SOMEONE STUFF THEIR MOUTH BEFORE

Animal House (cheeseburger); *Monty Python's The Meaning of Life* (every dish on menu); *Cool Hand Luke* (eggs); *I Love Lucy* (chocolates); any pie-eating contest scene (pies); *Fun with Dick and John* (dick).

HOW YOU CAN USE THIS IN YOUR REAL LIFE

Let's say you work in an office. You have nothing else in your life, really, except for this animal-calendar distribution office. You're also fat, which doesn't help matters. You normally go out to lunch with "the guys." Sometimes you go to Taco Bell, sometimes you go to that new place with the big-titted waitress with the gap teeth — either way, the point is you have a routine. Routines are boring, according to most scientific studies. This comedy "McNugget" gives you a chance to both change your routine, make some money, and be more popular than ever! Here's how:

1. Announce in the office that on Friday, at lunch, you're going to eat burritos until you puke (or until lunch break is over).
2. Start a betting pool to see how many burritos people think it will take to make you lose it.
3. Get people to bet (people love to gamble).
4. As the anticipation builds (oh, it's important to do the first step on at least the Monday before), bask in the glory of all the people in the office who will now notice you.
5. On Friday, at lunch, eat as many burritos as you can till you puke (or until the lunch break is over).
6. Afterward, collect money from bettors.
7. The next Monday, you will be the most popular guy in the office. Just remember to keep smiling as people engage you in conversation with admiration, saying "Wow, I can't believe you ate that many burritos!" and "Were you sick all weekend from the number of burritos you ate on Friday?"

No matter what happens, there will be lots of laughs and recognition, which is something you need.

#38 — ELABORATE DISGUISES

Just remember: it's not you in a disguise – it's your character. Believe it or not, this is a big source of confusion among non-comedians in milking this bit. Also a good opportunity for accent work; use primarily with a #16 (Clowns), #47 (Foreigner/Ethnics), #55 (Hiding in a Costume Shop), and a tangential #106 (Portraying an animal).

WHERE YOU'VE SEEN IT BEFORE

Mel Brooks's *Blazing Saddles* featured a High-larious© scene where a black man was dressed as a KKK member. The KKK is an organization dedicated to subjugating the black population (as well as Catholics, Jews, and anyone else who is not them). Mel Brooks, a notoriously short, funny Jew, was actually making fun of the KKK using this bit! If you can find your own racist organization to make fun of via elaborate comedic disguises, you'll be quite popular.

> **COMEDY FACT!**
>
> Legendary silent film comedian Buster Keaton was an alcoholic who ended his career making teen beach pictures that starred pop idol Frankie Avalon.

#39 — ENTRANCES / EXITS

Audiences love a "splashy" entrance and an "awesome" exit. With entrances, the Personal Theme Song (#99) is your best bet. For a great exit, try leaving with your pants down (#159 (Underwear)) or clumsily (#80 (Mr. Clumsy)) trip over something on your way out which brings the house down into rubble.

Make this the best part of your show! The audience deserves it!

PRIMO ENTRANCE EXAMPLE

"THE LENNY & SQUIGGY"* (from TV's *Laverne and Shirley*)
Check this out…

> **SHIRLEY:** "Here's the plan: we need to convince somebody to pretend they're <u>us</u> at work so we can go to the Sha Na Na concert!"
>
> **LAVERNE:** "It'll never work, I tell ya! Only an <u>idiot</u> would even attempt it…"
>
> *(Lenny and Squiggy suddenly burst through the front door.)*
>
> **SQUIGGY:** "Hello!" (Read: We're your idiots!)

*The most famous of sitcom producer Garry Marshall's patented writer-saving "entrance routines." Many of his creations would enter in the exact same way in <u>every</u> episode. Indeed, The Fonzie would strut onstage <u>whenever</u> the word "cool" was uttered – regardless of whether it was used as slang or in reference to temperature. Also used at every known performance of Lenny & the Squigtones.

EASY HOME USES – E & E

MEN: ENTRANCE

"Wifey" will love it when you come home from work and burst through the front door just as she's talking about penile-erection dysfunction.

WOMEN: EXIT

After a heated argument, stern "Hubby" will guffaw loudly when you angrily slam the door behind you, which somehow (we don't have all the answers) launches a pile of dog shit onto a framed picture of his asshole mother-in-law.

#40 — EXCESSIVE VOMITING, FARTING, BLEEDING, CRYING, SPITTING, & BURPING.

The more the better! Special effects can help in some cases; i.e. hot dogs make good fingers or penises ("excessive bleeding"), and projectile vomiting is a plus in any scene. Some say this bit is "disgusting," but we say that the laughter evoked from constant farting is the "glue of humanity."© At a very young age we all learn how absolutely hilarious bodily functions are; it's what binds kids with societal differences together. Would the warring tribes of Africa still want to immobilize their enemies in flaming rubber tires after watching Mr. Creosote (the fat guy) vomiting in the restaurant scene from *Monty Python's Meaning of Life*? We think not.

WHERE YOU'VE SEEN IT BEFORE

Where HAVEN'T you?

NO, SERIOUSLY, WHERE YOU'VE SEEN THIS BEFORE
- *Monty Python and The Holy Grail* – bleeding Black Knight
- *SNL* Julia Child Cuts Herself Sketch – bleeding Julia Child (Dan Aykroyd)
- *Dumb and Dumber* – the extended shitting scene (a variant)
- Monty Python's Sam Peckinpah's "Salad Days"

HALL OF FAME

Blazing Saddles – campfire scene. Done. The political ramifications of this classic are greatly underrated. Would there be a war in the Middle East if all the sheiks and rabbis got together and reenacted this scene at some Camp David revue??

(If you haven't seen this movie, then please PUT THE BOOK DOWN RIGHT AWAY and go rent it at your local video store. If you can't find it, then look some more. You idiot.)

#41 — EXCUSES

Minimum two-person bit due to the need to have a person to give the excuse to.

Listen, much of comedy is based in dishonesty, and you can't have a good excuse bit unless its foundation is a bed of lies. Face it, we all lie, we all come up with excuses every day – not to go to work, not to pick up the dry cleaning, not to have sex. The CHALLENGE to you is to make it FUNNY!

We recommend having an "excuse notebook" (similar to your notebook for Barbs, Comebacks, etc). Fill the book with "excuses" cross-referenced with scenarios cross-referenced with physical manifestations, and then apply them to the situation as needed.

SAMPLE COMEDY BIT FOR A #114 (ROMANTIC COMEDY) FILM

Let's say you've been asked by your boyfriend or girlfriend to go to a fancy dinner at his or her parents' house celebrating a big important occasion. But that sounds stupid, and you don't want to go. Here is one comedy response option (oh, the REAL reason you don't want to go is that you're having the boys/girls over to smoke some weed and watch the "big game"):

1. Call your "significant other"© and pretend like you have a cold, but don't call it a cold! Say you've come down with "something."
2. When pressed about the severity of this "something," remember to sneeze a lot.
3. If he/she is still unconvinced, then go into an overly long story about how you contracted this disease, heightening the absurdity at each turn. Make it so unbelievable that the only logical response from the other party is the patented (pending) "Well, I guess you must be sick, because that story is SO unbelievable, NO ONE could make it up! Get better soon, so we can have sex."
4. This is a good result; however, this will require that you come up with an excuse not to have sex.
5. At the end of the film, either the couple gets together with an understanding that they won't move forward in their relationship if it includes lying or they both find true happiness with seemingly minor characters.

#42 — EXERCISING

Very funny to watch fat people do this. Also funny to watch old people do practically nothing and get very tired.

#43 — EXTENDED DIRECTIONS

Once again, proof that comedy involves "listening." This age-old bit of "Hillbilly Hilarity"© came into its own during the classic TV comedy, *Green Acres,* much to the frustration of "Olivah," who always seemed to end up back at the same place! And always talking to that very same, straw-sucking, toothless rube!

HOW YOU CAN USE THIS IN YOUR REAL LIFE

Let's say you work in an office. And let's say that you are having a party, but you haven't invited Bill from the mailroom because let's say the last time you invited Bill to a party at your place he shit in your sheets. So somehow, Bill finds out about the party from William in the mailroom and awkwardly brings it up to you in the lunchroom. What do you say? Well, this is a perfect time to tell Bill that you moved and then give him a LONG LIST of directions to your "new" house… only you give him the WRONG directions that land him in the gang-infested part of town! The story gets even better when you all find out after the weekend that Bill never made it home that night. This is a golden opportunity for you to become what we call "popularly feared." No one will trust you anymore, but you'll be the funniest guy at the party once you tell people how you put one over on Bill!

#44 — FACIAL EXPRESSIONS

We take this opportunity to highlight the linchpin of facial comedy... ANGER FACES! Happiness, sadness, melancholiness – all have their place in the brave world of humor. However, registering anger is the cornerstone of most of the important comedy numbers. Wrath, rage, fury, hatred, impatience, irritation, craziness, getting your dander up, the slow burn, storming off in a "huff" – none of these could be performed successfully without good anger faces. Works well with the foil, the straight man, landlord characters, authority types in pursuit (car chases), "drill sergeant" sketches, etc.

YOU CAN EASILY WORK ON THIS IN FRONT OF YOUR HOME MIRROR

Begin by lowering your eyebrows. Now try one eyebrow down and one up. Now narrow your eyes – squint, even. Frown a little. Bare your teeth. Shake your head slightly. Now shake your head a lot. Throw in a "grrr!" noise. There are endless variations!

SITUATIONS WHERE YOU CAN PRACTICE YOUR "ANGER FACE"

- When someone pees too close to you at the trough in the ballpark men's room.
- After an old lady in front of you has 13 items in the 12 item express line.
- After a drug deal goes poorly for you.
- When your doctor tells you that you have ball cancer.
- After you get really raped.
- After your wife scratches your new car with the metal studs sewn onto her jeans.

WHY THIS IS A FUNNY FACE

OTHER FUNNY FACE OPTIONS
Tongue sticking out
Missing teeth
Marty Feldman eyes
Throwing a "Gookie"
Puffed cheeks
Infected piercings
Drool of any kind
Tongue touching eye
Chewed food on tongue
Vomiting
Vomit-through-nose laugh
Eye tic

HAT NO SANE PERSON
WOULD WEAR

RAISED
EYEBROWS

MUSSED HAIR

CROSS-EYES

HEAD TILTED LIKE
CURIOUS ANIMAL

SIMPLETON'S
OVERBITE

THE WRINKLE-LESS
SKIN OF A MAN-CHILD

VIEW FROM 6 FT. AWAY

NOSE OPTIONS
Runny nose
Finger in nose
Alternating flaring nostrils
Pulling on nose hair
Making "pig nose"
Tongue touching nose
Bloody nose
Bloody sneeze

#45 — FAKE VOMIT, SHIT, URINE, BLOOD, ETC.

If you've been drinking real urine for laughs, then we got to you just in time!!! Just thinking about it makes me absolutely sick. Here, finally, are the secrets of the trade revealed! The behind-the-scenes tricks that will allow you to... blugh... urmph... I'm sorry... I can't get that urine image out of my head... the behind-the-scenes tricks that will allow you to put one over on the audience and convince them you're actually eating excrement! The... I can't go on with this... the ruses that Hollywood employs to make you think someone's penis has been severed! The sketch-show illusion that convinces you... please... convinces you an actor can bleed for 10 minutes! And Benny Hill's dirty little secret for spitting out a mouthful of teeth! Yes, here are the cheats for duplicating pus, regurgitation, and greasy facial blemishes! At last, the kingdom of comedy is yours! ...I think I'm going to retch.

SUGGESTED EFFECTS

- Vomit / chunky beef stew and/or split-pea soup
- Shit / chocolate pudding
- Urine / yellow soda-pop beverage
- Blood / water and red food coloring
- Penis / hot dog; dildo; wiffle-ball bat
- Eyes exploding / creamer packets
- The human body / a dummy
- Breasts / balloons; surgery
- Spitting teeth / mints
- Cream pie / toxic shaving cream

Note: Beware of the backstage prankster who will substitute the real item for the fake! I'd kick his fucking ass! Seriously, kick the dude's ass.

#46 — FART NOISE

The more serious the situation, the funnier; e.g. bris, State of the Union Address, cancer-cure launch, hostage negotiations, coronation. Differs from a #40 in that we're not talking about excessiveness, no siree, we're talking about the well-placed toot. The single rip that breaks up a heart/lung transplant. Ahhhh.

This number is AMAZINGLY portable – take it anywhere.

OFFICIAL FART NAMES

Some of the industry-standard names include, but are not limited to: The Squirter, The Cricket, The Nixon, Dead Man's Nose, The Gas Leak, The Smell of the Edmund Fitzgerald, Big Ben, The Scorcher (popular with those with cigarette lighters handy), Rip Van Stinkle, The Grim Reaper, The Cagney and Lacey, Is It or Isn't It?, and End Game.

CAN I DO THIS AT HOME?

Sure, if you'd like.

#47 — FOREIGNERS / ETHNICS

Listen, we know that as of the time this book is written, everyone hates the US of A. We get that. But the world needs to see that we're not just a bunch of white guys running this country. (Except for all the presidents ever.) The rest of the world needs to see that we are a "melting pot of funny."© Sadly, we think that all those other foreign folks think that we just want to make them watch *The O.C.* (if you're reading this after 2007, you might have to look up this reference) and corrupt their lives. Well, cheer up friend! We believe that the "Comedy Tide" is turning quickly and any year now, we'll show the world that comedy can heal us all.

For now, though, we thought you should know who the funniest foreigners were in case you need to use some stereotypes in your comedy bits. Here's your handy factual reference guide:

FUNNIEST FOREIGNERS AND THEIR ATTRIBUTES*

- Chinese – bad drivers, short, speech is funny, very smart.
- Japanese – bad drivers, short, speech is funny, very smart, love cameras (or is that the Chinese?).
- Mexicans – big families, short, speech is funny, work at anything, smarter than we think.
- Slavs – big families, husky, speech is funny, work at anything, impossibly stupid.
- Russkies – still commies, speech is funny, crafty.

*Jews are no longer included in any scientific survey of "funniest ethnicities" because they are in a class by themselves! See #63.

#48 — FUNNY COMPLAINT LETTERS

Monty Python's Flying Circus (the TV show) is the #48 bible – so be warned: <u>any</u> attempt at a #48 will, right or wrong, be compared to that landmark program. Our advice? It ain't worth it. But if you're the type to say "Eat it, COMEDY BY THE NUMBERS! I'm doin' it anyway!", then at least perform it without a British accent. And remember, it's <u>your</u> funeral. (Seriously, do you think someone's gonna actually say to you "Dude, that was way funnier than <u>John Cleese</u>"? Get real.)

HOW YOU CAN USE THIS IN YOUR REAL LIFE

Let's say you work in an office. Actually you work in the customer-service department (maybe you see where THIS is going already!). There is probably no shortage of letters that you see written to your company from the people who have used your company's goods and/or services, but were somehow dissatisfied by what they received. Now's a chance to show the rest of the company how witty you are! Take one of the handwritten letters home. Practice copying the handwriting of the person who wrote it. Get it down EXACTLY. After a couple of weeks, you should be ready to mark up that letter so that it will seem as if the person who originally wrote the letter is CRAZY! For example, you can take a word from the original letter like "hit" and put an "s" in front! OR you can take a word like "small" and write "cock" after it. Then (and here's the best part) you put the letter up on the employee bulletin board in the lunchroom, and when people laugh at how outrageous the letter is, you explain what you did to make it funny. You might have to stand there all day to explain it to people, but it will totally be worth it!

SPECIAL MENTION REQUIRED

We'd like to take this opportunity to commend Mr. Lazlo Toth, a man with a dream. Although we don't agree with his politics (he liked Nixon – not us, though!), we believe that he is a shining example to all Americans (go, USA!) for his sticktoitiveness and determination. We'd like to spiritually, if not physically, reimburse him for all the postage money he's spent over the years keeping an eye on corporate America and our leaders. You go, Lazlo!

#49 — FUNNY EYEWEAR / FAKE TEETH / PHONY WARTS

This number isn't subtle. It might seem stupid to you and all your Harvard Lampooners, but use #49 without hesitation or apology and you'll reap long, rewarding laughs, as if to say, "Fuck words!"

#50 — FUNNY NAMES

Although this comedy staple goes all the way back to the Bible (Jehosaphat, anyone?!?), having this in your arsenal will laff-rantee© that you're a hit. You'll find that getting laughs with a funny name is as easy as taking a baby. Brace yourself securely for the almost tidal-like wave of guffaws headed your way upon utterance.

EXAMPLES FOR YOU TO USE — FREE!

Jabbermeyer Hoox, Nigel Poot, Bill Communist, Dick, Crackersnatch Pancyfancer, Snacklejack H. Squirtgoit, President Bush, Johnny Shitpants, Princess Gertrude, Timmy (with anything), Balnude Slobodnik, Richard Nixon, Nancy Asshole, Regent Carfloy Specklejekyll, Fifi La' Donk, Phil Brimmmmmmmmmmmm, The Rock, Pappercut Nicklestick, General Math, Castagu Bifolder, Phyllis the Lesbian, Vicardial Vavoom, Chief Running Water, Niles Toxic, Jackerphaffer Twab, anything with Fuckface, Enebrio, Baldisnatch Gunsowers, Queen Wideload, Chorkmafaw Jimmers, Snotjob Bammerblander, Chauncy, Kevin Ferguson, Madam Toot, Sweetie Pie, The Duke of Puke, Todd Cumstain.

HALL OF FAME

Cartoonist Don Martin's Fester Bestertester.

A MESSAGE FROM "YOU"

"Sure," you're saying, *"these funny names are funny, AND names, but what if I'm not on a TV show or a stand-up comedian? I can't just walk into a florist's and say 'My name is Chorkmafaw Jimmers!'"* Well, HERE'S an easy way to employ #50 in your OWN home! Household pets are readymade for comedic baptism. Dinner parties immediately liven up when you're overheard bellowing to your dog, "Sir Itches-a-lot! On the paper!"

And let me 'tell ya, chicks dig a dude who owns a porcupine with a silly moniker (Another Comedy Dating Tip!).

SAMPLE FUNNY PET NAMES TO GET YOU STARTED

Toodles, Jim-Jams, Puker, Little Asshole the Goldfish, Jonathan Livingston Tickfarm, Shit Hunter, Reginald, Fitsy, Mrs. Drool, Puddles, Piddler, Lazy, Dummo, Tinkler, Gandhi, Scriffy-Scruffs, Scraffy-Scriffs, Scrammy-Scrums, Ol' Rabies Bait, Lil' Miss Eats Everything, Dick-sniffer, Dr. Horseflies, Scabby the Cow, Bouncer, Mr. Licks, Cloppity, The Hair Machine, Bumpy-Wumpy the Bastard Turtle, Heaves, Heaves Jr., Lady Heaves, Reek, Wags the Indescribable Disaster, Thomas, Murderer, Nibbles, The Shed of State, Fatso-boy, Your Majesty.

Little Asshole the Goldfish (left)

TIP!
Comedy Killers — Beware

In your valiant effort to make the world smile, you will unfortunately have to face several obstacles, or "Comedy Killers," along the way. These can include everything from a jealous boyfriend to a recent global tragedy. Try to situate yourself in humor-friendly environments at all times!

COMEDY KILLERS - FOR "PROFESSIONALS"

- Expensive sets
- Reading cue cards
- Notes from executives
- Unfunny scripts
- No jokes
- Big budgets
- No on-set trailer

COMEDY KILLERS - IN YOUR EVERYDAY LIFE

- Sweating
- Over-use of your tongue
- Beady eyes
- Unfunny fidgeting
- Excessive eye drool
- An attention-grabbing lip blister

The only known cure for comedy death:
#159 (Underwear)

#51 — FUNNY PERSON PLAYING A MUSICAL INSTRUMENT

If you're multi-talented (one of the talents being comedy), then you just might be able to pull off this bit. Most people start off taking music lessons when they're little kids and then add comedy lessons later. Unless you become one of those longhaired rockers (the kind that get groupies for a couple of years), you should know that most people find that music has no real advantage in their lives. BUT if you start to combine a music talent WITH comedy at an early age, then you really could become popular. Just ask Victor Borge!!

We suggest studying the greats of this combo-genre, but beware: Every Marx Brothers comedy movie was brought to a screeching unfunny halt by Chico and Harpo's insistence on having a music break for them to "show off" their "other talent" (or in Harpo's case, "only"). Don't fall into their trap!

BUT ARE THERE GOOD EXAMPLES FOR ME TO FOLLOW?

Currently as we sit here and write this book, the "musicomedy" field is dominated by Tenacious D and, well, that's it: Tenacious D. And the "D" is just naturally funny — they ain't even trying! Back in the '70s, the BeeGees experimented with doing comedy sketches during their stadium shows, but their timing was said to be poor and Robin refused to look stupid. Before that, Jack Benny used his violin as a psychological crutch to escape the memories of a childhood of "torture." Henny Youngman also carried a violin on stage and was quite good musically. Using a classic #30 (Double entendre), he once referred to his playing as "fingering his instrument."

THIS IS THE PERFECT NUMBER FOR YOU IF YOU'RE LOOKING TO BE "DIFFERENT." GOOD LUCK WITH THAT.

COMEDY SIDENOTE: Henny's prowess at cocksmanship led to a lifelong rivalry with Milton Berle and *F-Troop*'s Forrest Tucker for the affection of anything with a pussy.

#52 — FUNNY SLANG

Been around since there was language to be slanged. Some examples good for everyday use: "danger hole" (for vagina); "pillowlicious" (for dreamy); "spanglish banana slam dancer" (all-purpose substitute for gays). Make up your own and send it to us!

HOW YOU CAN USE THIS IN YOUR REAL LIFE

Let's say you work in an office. This is an office that manages the flow of blank DVDs between China (where they're made) and your East Coast branch. Your company gets the blank DVDs and then sells them to the Japanese so they can record American movies illegally. It's complicated, but you have a mortgage, so you don't complain much. Also, your office just happens to be one of those offices where people send out memos all day "cc-ing" everyone. Crazy. Well here's your chance to introduce some funny slang and pass it off as "office lingo." (Imagine getting the CEO of your company to refer to the men's room as the "pissatorium"— I bet you can do it!) Here's a simple exercise: Next time you go to a meeting, offer to record the "meeting minutes" for everyone. After the meeting, type up a meeting minutes memo that accurately describes the discussion as well as decisions that were made; HOWEVER, before you send it out to everyone, change some of the phrases! For example:

[*Actually said in the meeting:*]

"The next shipment of DVDs will arrive in January by freighter packed in standardized wood crates."

[*What you write in the meeting minutes:*]

"The new D-LOAD is SUNRISING in the KING MONTH and coming by POPPABOAT in some TREE BABIES."

EVERYONE who gets that memo will crack up! Except maybe for the Chinese, who aren't familiar with "meeting-minute humor."

#53 — GOSSIP

Staple "foil" character. Mrs. Kravitz, the nosey neighbor from the TV show *Bewitched* set the standard. Usually a female character; however, add this to a scene in which a group of tough football players are crocheting and "dishing" and you'll actually sense the audience looking for some knees to slap.

Writing.

COMEDY GOSSIP

Comedy is ever changing. And knowledge is power. And secrets are fun. Therefore, as in <u>any</u> heavy industry, in order to stay on top of things you <u>must</u> "make the scene" whenever possible (stand-up clubs; improv houses; sitcom tapings; riff sessions), if only to see what your peers are passing off as "jokes." We regret to say, being cooped up in our respective apartments for the last few days (in order to write this book for you), your precious authors have had little time to hang out with our comedy friends/opponents (see picture above). Yes, we're a little behind on "what's doing" out there. And so… now it's time to roll out the red carpet for the COMEDY BY THE NUMBERS© Style & Gossip columnist: Mr. Bitch Somerset!

The Beat

by Bitch Somerset

Wahoo! Hello cowboys and girls! Bitch here, with the latesy and the greatsy in the gay (the traditional meaning) world of komedy. ITEM: What young cut-up was "scene" using PROPS at his Aspen Comedy Festival set, much to the chagrin of his B. Hills oh-so-stuffy handlers? I'll give you a hinty-winty: he's got a mouth I'd like to stick my penis into. WHOOPS! Did I write that out loud? You naughty fingers! Ta! ITEM: Which stitch-com actress(!) is sooo Obsessioned with Lucille Ball(s) she's taken to smoking eight packs a day?! Here's a cluesy-woozy: it isn't "_all_ of them." Word is she's also fretting over her Cuban's "missile crisis!" More 'splainin' less complainin', perhaps? Only in komedy! Ta! And when did a "tight 5" become a "tight 25"? Jest asking. You know who I miss? The enigmatic Unknown Comic. Lourde knows I need a masked man to kome and whisk me away on his giant deed-steed! I've been saddled with the Rule of 3s lately! Ohhh, I'm so fucking horny for celebrities!! OOPSY! I've got a case of the naughty fingeers, what can I say.

On my horizon

WHAT'S HOT!
Anything Ben Stiller
Will Ferrell's wig choices
Dribble glasses
Amy Poehler's dead-to-rights Wacko Jacko
The lav mics at the Joke Hut

WHAT'S NOT!
Sound cues at Tickle's
Yahoo Serious (I'm so sorry, 'Hoo)
Looooong pauses
The Imogene Coca sandwich at Lindy's
Phunny

Up-and-comer Seth is a kid to watch. Catch him nightly in the parking lot of Popeye's Chicken on Santa Monica Blvd.

FIVE MINUTES AGO:
Little Nellie's "Little House" jokes – sorry, A****! But I know you'll _Landon_ your feet again!

(Masks from my personal collection.)

"Does the wife know, Henny?"

"I know where he stores the hammer."

"A great 'improviser' - -if you know what I mean."

This has been Bitch Somerset and you're not and that's the truth and excuuuse me! Ta!

-B*

#54 — GROUP OF PEOPLE ENTERING / EXITING AN AREA THAT COULDN'T LOGICALLY HOLD THEM

Speaks for itself. This bit was tested and re-tested in Stockholm at the turn of the century and then shamelessly pirated by the Ritz Brothers in Vaudeville.

GOOD EXAMPLES

- Marx Brothers's *A Night at the Opera* – the stateroom scene. This famous scene was also a sly commentary on a major social issue of the day – illegal immigration. The movie studio chose to deliver their anti-immigration point of view by means of having the Marx Brothers pack too many people, all with different agendas, into a space too small for them. In the end the room exploded, much the way America could explode if too many of the "wrong" kind of people are invited in. Not so funny, now that we think about it.
- Circus clown cars.
- Pro-lifers at an abortion clinic.

#55 — HIDING IN A COSTUME STORE

One of several numbers that regularly utilizes the genius "chased by gangsters" set-up, where the threat of violence is turned on its head for comedic effect.

HERE'S A SCENARIO FOR YOU TO USE

1. You are a fat man.
2. You've just mistakenly been caught in bed with the mob boss's moll (who has huge tits – not totally necessary, but good for following-along purposes).
3. You jump out a window onto a fire escape while the mob boss's triggermen go down the front stairs.
4. You race down the street with these two button men running behind you.
5. All of a sudden you duck into a costume shop.
6. You run past the teenage checkout boy who looks up from his *CRACKED* magazine and says: "Hey, mister..."
7. You disappear into the backroom.

8. The two goombahs run into the store and stop to look around for you.
9. They ask the teenage boy if he's seen a short balding guy with a mustache and blue boxers run into the store.
10. The kid murmurs "no" out of fear of being involved.
11. Just as the two Italianish mob hitmen are about to leave, scratching their heads because they can't find you, you walk by dressed like Marilyn Monroe from *The Seven-Year Itch* – white dress, wig, and everything.
12. Without looking too closely, they step aside for you to pass, their eyes grazing over your hefty bosom.
13. You say "thank you" in a voice that you believe approximates that of Marilyn Monroe when she was alive.
14. They tip their hat and smile as if they want to nail you.
15. As the door jingles for you on the way out, one of the wiseguys says to the other, "Did you see the mustache on that dame?"... The other one says, "Heyyyy, that was no dame!"... That's when the double-take kicks in, their hats fly up in the air, and they take off running for the door.

OTHER COSTUME-SHOP DISGUISES

- French whore
- Front half of horse
- Prune farmer
- Aunt Jemima

GOOD #3 (ANTI-COMEDY) DISGUISE TO PULL OUT OF THE RACKS

- A mask of your own face.

COMEDY FACT!

George Carlin has, at times during his career, had both long hair and very short hair.

#56 — HIPPIES

Bob Hope was the first to point out what was funny about hippies – their huge egos. If you want to include this character in your comedy, it's best to read up as much as you can in old textbooks about hippies. Always approach real hippies with caution, especially when seeing them at museums or in head shops or in your apartment selling you drugs.

WHERE YOU'VE SEEN IT BEFORE

George Carlin is a classic example of a "hippie" comedian who is often so high that he doesn't know what he's saying. Also Gallagher has long hair. This bit couldn't exist without the Vietnam War.

LOCATIONS WHERE THE INTRODUCTION OF THE HIPPIE CHARACTER IS MOST LIKELY TO GET A LAUGH

Operating theater, WWI treaty-negotiation scenes, *Inherit the Wind* parodies, heavyweight fights, bead-factory assembly lines, NASA brainstorming sessions, roller-derby training films, spelling bees for the elderly.

#57 — HUMOR FUNNY TO GAYS

They love the ass-play stuff, but studies have shown they will actually laugh like "other" people! If you're reading this and you're a gay (first off, thank you!), you might just want to skip to something more fun than the analysis of your brand of comedy. For you non-gays (thank you too!), just realize that there is often a secret code among the gay people that is hard for normal people to learn. This extends to comedy, similar to the way dogs can hear certain frequencies that humans can't. It's weird, but then again, being gay is weird too – we mean, "funny" weird!

The authors are not gay, but consider themselves brave enough to include this brand of comedy on the likelihood that you or someone you know is gay and will get a kick out of having some gay stuff in the book. We love you, Nathan Lane! Love! You!

HALL OF FAME

Wayland Flowers and Madam – freakiest sideshow act ever.

FAMOUS GAYS

Elton, Rock, Barney, Martina, Scott, Jm. J, Oscar, Tony, Truman, Terry, Ellen, Rosie, Melissa, Portia, Gertrude, Alice, Carson, Nathan, Gore – oh, there are lots of them.

GOOD GAY NAMES FOR YOU TO USE IN YOUR COMEDY (OR REAL) LIFE

Any of the above, Bruce, Brucie, Bryce.

comedy classics collector's stamps

CLIP 'EM AND COLLECT 'EM!

CAUTION: Make sure stamp is completely cut out before using.

#58 — ILLNESSES, AFFLICTIONS, MALADIES

This was originally a comedic avenue only open to the Europeans. English scribes in particular wrote many a farce based on the sickly. The era of the black plague was also, ironically, the time of the greatest explosion of avant-garde stage comedy man has ever seen. Playwrights, who are notorious shut-ins, were able to survive the legions of lesions that surrounded them and write... and boy did they ever. The human condition gave them their inspiration, and to this day, most theater historians believe that without the bubonic plague, theater as we know it would have been reduced to musicals about cats. Millions died so that theater might live, and this book is a salute to their spirit.

On the hilarious side, the pilgrims, who introduced the "diseased blanket" comedy prop to our native society in the late 17th century, would be proud to know how their little starter bit has fostered a whole industry that includes fake puke and the phony bald cancer wig *(see #86 – Novelty Items)*.

LITTLE KNOWN FACT: Those who are physically different than us, or in an inordinate amount of pain, find no greater thrill and pride than when they are the source of a comedian's or character's jokes. If you are lucky enough to have an audience with someone in a wheelchair, don't hesitate to point that out to the rest of the crowd! "They" love being "picked on!"

WHERE YOU'VE SEEN IT USED COMEDICALLY BEFORE
- *My Left Foot*
- *Terms of Endearment*
- *The Ringer*
- *There's Something About Mary*
- *Brian's Song*

#59 — IMPOSSIBLE DISTANCES IN A SHORT TIME

A visual comedic device often thought to have originated in the tales of the Mongol hordes who crossed into China at an unheard-of pace. Not originally funny at the time due to the raping and pillaging and whatnot, but can be used in modern-day comedy as part of the Take Family (#143-148). With careful editing, a mother-in-law-showing-up-at-the-door-right-after-your-crying-wife-hangs-up-the-phone bit will not only guarantee laughs, but gasps and seat-peeing as well.

#60 — IMPROVISATION / IMPROV / IMPRO

Screw that! Plan ahead. You know everyone else does. "*The Unprepared Comedian is like a cigarette without a lighter. I'm totally serious.*" –Dr. Hoffman (**COMEDY BY THE NUMBERS**)

IF YOU ARE GOING TO MOVE AHEAD WITH THE MAKE'M UPS

Improvisation is both an art and a non-art. That is what we've learned from our years in the biz. There are those who believe that you can get a bunch of people to pay good money to watch a bunch of other people make up stuff as they go along. And then there are others who believe that the first group of people are idiots and that the make'm ups should be done in private until they become "for-sure funny" words and THEN the people will pay to see GUARANTEED comedy. If it reads confusing, that's because it is.

We don't really care if you learn to improvise or not; the main thing is that if you're going to do it, then have a good name for your group so you don't have to feel god-damn embarrassed every time someone asks you what you're doing.

Here are some really good group names mixed in with names to avoid – let's see if you can tell the difference!

- Half Serious
- Titular Head
- Tequila Mockingbird
- Born to be Mild
- The Envelope, Peas
- Spare Farts
- Bassprov
- That's Infotainment!
- The Make'm Ups
- The Fast and the Curious
- Fist Full of Irony
- Fish Shtick
- John Cougar Mellencamp
- Texas Joke'm
- Laugh, Wince, Repeat
- Baby-Back Ribbers

#61 — INAPPROPRIATE BEHAVIOR

This is the foundation for comedy throughout the world. Almost any-thing funny is by definition inappropriate. Use this number in any sit-uation where people think something should be happening a certain way – and you do it another way. The great example is in the *Mary Tyler Moore Show* episode called "Chuckles the Clown" – Mary can't stop laughing at the funeral of a clown. Wholly inappropriate, but fucking high-larious!© Act inappropriately and you can't lose!

SIDENOTE: The British spell it "behaviour" – they're always trying to be difficult.

HOW YOU CAN USE THIS IN YOUR REAL LIFE

Let's say you work in an office. If it's like most offices, then there is an accepted way to act and dress. To use this inventive number, start by doing things differently than the accepted way. For example, lots of offices have "Casual Fridays," where people come in to work with-out ties and/or wearing denim jeans. Well, you will get lots of laughs when you show up for work on a "CF" in a formal dinner jacket and a pretentious scarf! Everyone will be attracted to you and admire your bravery. Also, most offices have an employee refrigerator for sand-wiches, leftovers, and Jenny Craig lunches. Here's what you do: First trap and kill a pig. You'll see that this is a great opportunity for you to get some laughs by bringing in a huge roasted pig's head and put-ting it in the fridge. Bring the pig's head out at lunch and tear into it with your hands only – and just watch your coworkers' heads shake in laughing disapproval! They might even say out loud, "Oh, that (your name here); he's always doing funny inappropriate things!"

COMEDY FACT!

Freddie Prinze committed suicide after the second season of the hit TV show *Chico and the Man*. He was replaced by a child actor.

TIP!

The Name Game... if you want to go "pro"

Using COMEDY BY THE NUMBERS© is important, actually vital, to your becoming a comedian (or popular, which is often the same thing), but one of the things that we can't do for you with this book is give you a comedy name. Don't get us wrong... we could, but that would definitely be extra, and, given how many people we expect to help change their lives through this book, would become difficult and tiresome. But don't let our apathetic attitude stop you!

Before you start moving ahead with pictures and postcards promoting yourselves, take a step back and decide if you and your partner (or group) have the right "comedy names." Here are some "do's and don'ts" (although we're not actually calling them that):

- With duos, the straight man's name is traditionally listed first, funny man second. This is because in vaudeville and burlesque the straight man was considered the star of the act. (Interestingly, one of the first comedy teams was comprised of two straight men, Abbott and Burns. The act was billed as An Uproarious Night Of Questions With No Answers! *"Some of the best set ups we've ever seen"* —The Times.)
- Ethnic never hurts. Although, never get "too Jewy" or "too Black"
- Avoid puns for group names. Punny names will last about five minutes in the rough and tumble world of comedy posturing.
- Think about a name that will both get a laugh and get you laid.
- Non sequiturs are always a good idea, but avoid disease names like "Cancer Watch" or "The Cyst Boyz."
- Don't forget to ask anyone you meet what they think — their ideas are just as important as yours when it comes to your personal creativity and integrity.
- When you get really famous you can go back to using your real name like John Mellencamp and Sinbad.

BEWARE: A certain flow, a "rolling off of the tongue" if you will, is particularly crucial with team names. Yarnell and Shields, Chong and Cheech, the Brigade of Upright Citizens, the Pack of Rats, Brownshoe and Tenspeed, and Python, Monty — they all fail in this department... thank God they decided on Shields and Yarnell!

#62 — IRONY

Okay, let's be honest. You have to know what something is in order to figure out what would be ironic about it. There's a dictionary, probably, that will give you the exact definition, so we'll let you do that research for yourself. We'll try to point up some examples. For example, if you got a speeding ticket while driving over the speed limit to get to a court-ordered anti-speed driving class, that would be ironic. Just not funny. Your challenge is to find the humorous irony in a situation. It's tough.

**OTHER EXAMPLES THAT MIGHT BE HELPFUL
IN EXPLAINING HOW IRONY CAN BE FUNNY**

- An Orthodox Jew who keeps kosher inherits a Pork & Shrimp Farm from a long-lost relative.
- A Klu Klux Klan member discovers that he's black during a KKK talent show.
- After a prolonged fast for the sake of Mother India, M.K. Gandhi finally sits down to eat at a restaurant and the service is terrible.

The other variations of this word include "ironic" and "ironical."

#63 — JEWS & THEIR IDIOSYNCRACIES

If you're smart enough to have bought this book and read this far, then it won't surprise you when we definitively declare that the Jews are the funniest people in the world. Lots of people think that the blacks were funny because they were slaves. Well, let's set the record straight – it's not a contest, but historical documents prove that the Jews were by far the funniest slaves ever.

Important thing to know: ALL Jews EVERYWHERE are exactly like Woody Allen (famed filmmaker and alleged pedophile), and have the same opinions and character traits. Once you embrace this fact, you will be able to move forward without wasting energy on "re-inventing the Jew"© in your comedy world. Little hats are funny. Hanging sideburns are funny. Being cheap is funny. Really all you need to do is throw some typical character traits into your piece. Non-Jews will laugh at the Jewish characters because of deep-seated jealousy – and Jews love to laugh at themselves out of self-hate. So that's 100% of your audience… laughing!

WHERE AND WHEN DID JEWS GET TO BE SO FUNNY?

Ironically, the Jews were not "chosen" to be funny. The story is told through our elders that a group of them were passing through Rome in 3 B.C. and stopped to perform a series of silly songs for Pope Pius the XI. Before having them stoned to death, the Pope was said to remark, "Those little people with the noses amused me." Word spread.

GREAT THING ABOUT JEWS

Due to their history of moving around so much, the comedy of the Jews has proved greatly adaptable. Jews really can be used in any comedic sketch and it will be funny! Examples include: church confession scene, medieval joust bit, little-league team "win one for the kid with cancer" speech, etc.

FAMOUSLY FUNNY JEWS WHO HATE THEMSELVES SO MUCH IT'S FUNNY

- Woody Allen
- Albert Brooks
- Henry Kissinger

****FULL DISCLOSURE ALERT****

This book is considered "half-Jewish" in publishing circles due to the Hebraic heritage of co-author Dr. Gary Rudoren. (See Dr. Gary's Certificate of Ritual Circumcision, reprinted at the back of this book.)

#64 — KIDS DOING THINGS GROWN-UPS DO

Maybe YOUR gang could be… "Our Gang"! (Famed orphans trained to be funny during the Great Depression.) Imagine how funny it is when small children are placed in positions normally associated with adults. "Kiddie komedy,"[©] as we call it, was inadvertently created by the robber barons of the Industrial Age who exploited child labor to buy their gold mansions and whores. Little did they know they would also be creating one of the great comedic devices of the 20th century.

GREAT EXAMPLE THAT WE CAME UP WITH

Essentially, this bit turns common sense on its bald head. Picture a scene with a nervous woman going to see her gynecologist, perhaps to have a cyst removed (serious, huh?). While sitting there in her paper gown with her feet in the stirrups, the doctor walks in and we discover… HA… it's Macaulay Culkin! (Of the *Home Alone* era.) He looks down between her legs and then back up at the screen with his hands next to his face – High-larious![©]

WHAT IF I DON'T HAVE ACCESS TO CHILDREN?

There is no shortage of parents willing to introduce their children to the world of comedy at a young age. We recommend spending a lot of time at neighborhood playgrounds staring at children to figure out which ones will be the funniest and then approaching them directly with treats. They will then inform their parents about this great opportunity for their future.

FAMOUS PRECOCIOUSLY FUNNY CHILDREN
WHO GREW UP TO BE OLDER

- Danny "Partridge" Bonaduce
- Gary "Arnold" Coleman
- Robert "Mickey" Blake

SERIOUS REMINDER

Although pretty children are charming, it's preferable that the child be slightly disfigured or unusually fat, so the audience believes that laughing at the child is actually bolstering the child's self-image, however momentarily, and distracting him from the flaws that society will focus on for the rest of his life.

#65 — KILLING A PERSON

Funny if mistakenly done by adorable toddler. Can also be tragic.

BEFORE YOU THINK WE'RE INSENSITIVE

A famous Second City scene involves a funeral where a man has died trying to get the last bit of food out of a Van Kamps Bean Can. This sketch alone proves that there are funny ways to die or be killed.

DID YOU KNOW?

There is a whole writing cottage industry built around follow-ups to unusual screen deaths. Specially trained comedy writers coordinate with other sub-specialist murder writers in order to find JUST THE RIGHT follow-up to any given character's death scene. Possible examples:

- Super villain's henchman falls into a vat of trained sharks with chainsaws. (Hero can add a quip such as "Ooh, I bet he SAW that coming!")
- Hero injecting poison into a villain with a hypodermic needle. (This gives the hero an opportunity to use a quippy line like "Take that, you prick!")
- A guy (could also be non-villain) has a heart attack while having sex; crotchety old policeman who finds the body references that they should be on the look out for "killer pussy" (sometimes followed by a group laugh from heterosexual cops gathered about the body).

COMEDY FACT!

Curly, of Three Stooges fame, resented shaving his head because women found him less attractive.

#66 — KILLING A LOT OF PEOPLE

Seemingly not funny as well, and needs to be different than a hilarious #65. Sometimes just the threat of mass murder can be funny, a prime example being the national furor during the Cold War, when our fear of Communism needed the balance of gut-wrenching genocidal laughter. If you don't laugh at *Dr. Strangelove or How I Learned To Stop Worrying and Love The Bomb,* you're clinically dead. We're not saying that you have to go around thinking about killing a lot of people for laughs, but at least you're thinking about getting laughs, and that's ALWAYS a good thing!

HOW YOU CAN USE THIS IN YOUR REAL LIFE

You might be thinking we're nuts, but hear us out on this one. Let's say you work in an office. Your office happens to be NORAD and you're 3 miles below a mountain in Colorado. But you don't have just any job, like Accounts Receivable; no, your job is keeping an eye on a monitor that shows the movement of the Chinese Army massed along the Russian border. Pretty serious stuff, right? Well, it doesn't have to be! The odds are PRETTY slim that the Chinese are going to attack the Russians while you're staring at that little screen, don't you think? Why not have a little fun by pretending that you've intercepted some coded Chinese message from their "High Command"? Tell your coworkers that the Chinese communications are in a code ONLY YOU UNDERSTAND, so they have to believe you! One day, you say the Chinese are going to start throwing "pessimistic fortune cookies" over the border in order to break down the Russians' will. The fortunes tell them to convert to being Chinese or else the Chinese will "deliver" death to them – chop chop! Keep going with a story about how the Chinese have ordered 2 million ladders brought to the border so that they can scale the Russian fences. Tell your boss to tell the President that the Chinese said they'll be calling the U.S. for a big ladder order "any day now." Just keep making shit up until finally one of the generals down in NORAD asks you if you're making it up and then… then you start to smile and slowly build up to bursting out laughing! You hold your arms out with your wrists together and say "Guilty as charged, sir! Ya got me!"… Pretty soon all of NORAD will slowly start to laugh with you and you'll have wrung some great comedy from the near-Armageddon situation that YOU created! "Arm-a-geddin" outta here, indeed!

#67 — MAGIC

Bad magicians with odd names like "the great Masterbato!" doing incompetent magic can be funny as a bit, but beware making this character appear at all three-dimensional. There is in fact no such thing as magic, but a good magician character can be used in scenes with kids and for the amusement of #113s.

"The Great Bad-o!"

LITTLE-KNOWN FACT: Harry Houdini, famed magician and escape artist, was also the inventor of the "knock-knock joke."

COMEDY FACT!

Performance artist and avant garde "comedian" Andy Kaufman, who had hoped to fake his own death, was beaten to the punch by real death.

#68 — MAKING FUN OF SOMEONE ELSE'S FLAWS

Shy away from the obvious #113; it's the sign of a shallow comedian. However, it's good to keep a file going of people and what about them you could exploit, given the opportunity to do it publicly. However, this is not to be confused with racism. Race is not a flaw, people! This bit is on the razor's edge of being funny/being an asshole, but who cares. Don't be afraid to be an asshole – Dice Clay embraced this bit and look where he is today!

REMEMBER OUR OLD FRIEND, "SELF-HATE"

We've established by this point in the book that we know what we're talking about. So believe us when we tell you to be careful when applying this number. More than any other bit of comedy, #68 is a cry for help from that little-boy-who-peed-his-pants-in-the-school-play-while-dressed-as-a-pumpkin-because-he-forgot-his-lines-and-all-the-other-kids-teased-him-forever-til-he-took-an-AK-47-and-blew-them-away-during-homeroom inside all of us. You absolutely CAN get laughs making fun of other people's flaws, but, really, is that the kind of person you want to be? (We say "Yes!!")

HALL OF FAME

Don Rickles

HOW YOU CAN USE THIS IN YOUR REAL LIFE:

Let's say you work in an office. In that office there is one person who bugs the hell out of you. His name is Mort and he's the comptroller. No one is even sure what a comptroller is, but what really bugs you is that Mort insists on being copied on every memo that goes out of the office. Mort also happens to have a lazy eye and doesn't mind letting you know about it. He's always, "Me and my lazy eye can't pick up the check today." That's really aggravating, isn't it? Well, you can get your comedy revenge (and probably get in good with the rest of the folks in the office who hate "lazy eye Mort" too) by starting to wear an eyepatch to work. You will have one-upped Mort (#91) AND made him aware that you weren't going to take his BS anymore! Now YOU can be all, "Oh, I can't clean the coffee pot because of my eyepatch," and stuff like that. If your coworkers are like us, they'll laugh like crazy at the eyepatch bit.

#69 — MEDICATIONS AND THEIR SIDE EFFECTS

Suppositories are funny. It's a funny word and it's funny to think that you could shove something up your ass and it will make you feel better (sorry gay people). Big needles aren't funny, but the threat of a big needle, filled with anything, often will cause "comedic fainting." Here's the deal: We're all afraid to die and sometimes we go to extreme measures just to prolong our sad, pathetic lives (we're not talking about YOU). To that end, we reach out for whatever cures us and sometimes the cure is "laughter!" Remember, it's not usually the medicine itself that's funny — although the word "placebo" works as both a pseudo-medical term and a good name for a sexual position. Side effects can cause overreaction and overreactions can get you big laughs. LSD wasn't a funny medicine when it was used by the CIA to overthrow Castro (how'd that work out for you guys, CIA?), but became funny when some rogue agents turned it loose on the hippie population (#56) and they in turn made it funny with their free love and whatnot. We can't do any better than good old *Reader's Digest* when we say: "Laughter is the best medicine." Crazy *Reader's Digest*.

CLASSIC EXAMPLE

In a sketch from *The Carol Burnett Show,* actor Tim Conway is the dentist and foil Harvey Korman is the patient. Seemingly a professional dentist, mistakenly Tim sticks the Novocain into his hand instead of Harvey's mouth. The hand goes numb, becomes nearly unusable, and then due to this newfound numbness, Tim mistakenly (again!) sticks the needle (filled with more numbing Novocain) into his own forehead. Tim eventually acts like those parts of his body are numb and falls down. This scene was also funny to the actors who decided to use the innovative (for its time) "cracking up at yourself" method of comedy-sketch acting. Mr. Korman went on to teach this technique in workshops throughout the country and northern parts of Canada. Mr. Conway went on to make a series of successful workshop videos where he was on his knees as a little person (sly version of #36 (Dwarves, Midgets, and the Like)).

HOW YOU CAN TRY THIS AT HOME

First find some drugs and take too many of them. It's best to do this in front of other people who have promised you that they will take notes for you on how funnily you react to the drugs AND save you from dying if need be. Let us know how your hilarious "overdose" works out!

AND NOW, LET'S TAKE A COMEDY BY THE NUMBERS©
MOMENT FOR A COMEDY BY THE NUMBERS©
SALUTE TO HARVEY KORMAN

Quite honestly one of the best utility comedians ever, as seen in his work on *The Carol Burnett Show.* A perfect straight man, a master of accents and dialects and pin-sharp timing – these are the traits of the heroic utility comedian. Korman has also successfully delivered the rare "one-two comedy punch" in the films *Blazing Saddles* and *High Anxiety.* ALSO played consummate straight man Bud Abbott in the television bio-pic *Bud and Lou* (with Sir Buddy Hackett as "Lou"). Young utility comedians note: After you study Dan Aykroyd, study the Harv.

AND WHO COULD FORGET THE CLOWN PRINCE OF
UTILITY COMEDIANS, MAY HE REST IN FUNNY PEACE

Phil Hartman

#70 — MENSTRUATION

Finesse this hilarious number and every day will be your "time of the month" – for laugh 'em ups! While you can work funny quips into your everyday life, we'd like to give some tips to those stand-up comedy warriors:

If you're one of the gals, then you're guaranteed to get 51% of the audience to relate to you if you start talking about your "woman problems," AND you'll most likely get the other 49% (men) interested because of what we call "The Gina Factor." Studies have shown that men (well, except for the gay guys) react positively to any mention of the vagina (we shortened it to "gina" because it sounded cuter to us).

If you're one of the guys, then you're guaranteed to get 49% of your audience to be on your "side" when you make fun of the women's monthly ritual. The other 51% will probably laugh along, as they don't want to seem "too uptight." Again, 100% success! End every reference to how women are different while they're being visited by the "Gina Fairy" (we just made that up, but you can use it) with the word "...right?" It will be like an intimate conversation with the audience.

WHERE "BLEEDING GINA" REFERENCES WORK BEST

- Marriage proposal
- Women's Lib riot
- Circus press conference
- Technical-school graduation speech
- Slaughterhouse interview
- Puppet show
- Greek Orthodox wedding vows

HOW TO USE IT IN YOUR HOME (FOR MEN ONLY)

When the lady of the house is experiencing "cramps," simply whip out this gem:

> WIFE: "Ohhh, fuck! This shit is the worst fucking fuck pain I've ever– arrgh! I wanna goddam die! Fuck you! Get away from me! Blaaaaaaggh!!"
>
> YOU: "Yeah, it sucks." (*Then pretend to hit the TV remote (#88 - Object Work).*)

Your reward? A nod of approval from the missus, for you understand what she's going through. Now you can both share a laugh over the situation several days later.

#71 — MICKEY ROONEY

Famed child star who literally never grew up! The original "Mick" is never at a loss for stories that he himself is amused by. Inch for inch, ten times funnier than second-banana Brad Garrett (the funniest tall guy we've ever seen). Revered also for his "wife-count" and the fact that he banged Ava Gardner.

AUTHORS' NOTE

We really wanted to get a picture of Mr. Rooney for our book, but his estate wouldn't sell it to us. But our comedy history seems to be slipping through our nation's fat fingers. There are lots of outlets for comedy nowadays – TV, movies, the interweb, books (like this one), iPods, etc. But back in "the day," it was mostly movies and radio (okay, there were still books, vaudeville, and burlesque), and Rooney was one of the bright shining stars. We're STILL jealous of Mickey!

#72 — MICROPHONE BITS

If you've been doing your comedy mic-less all these years, there's a good chance that you've never been fully heard. **Little-known historical fact:** The microphone itself was responsible for one of the great wars in the 20th century. There are those who blame the rise of one Adolph Hitler and WWII on the invention of the mic. If Hitler hadn't been able to amplify his voice at all those huge rallies, so that the people in the back of the crowd could hear his "The Aryan race is the best... blah blah blah... let's go take over Poland... blah blah blah... I hate the Jews and you should too.... blah blah," then his followers would have most likely been limited to just the few Nazis in the front of the crowd and those in the back would have sulked away bitterly, like everyone who ever saw Milli Vanilli. But, on the good side, the mic helped comedy reinvent itself in the '40s, and we believe, just like Hitler did, that the people in the back of the room deserve to hear everything too!

Remember: You're never on stage alone as long as you've got a phallic mic in your hand.

MICROPHONE BITS THAT "WORK"

- Pretending the mic is an ice-cream cone
- Using the mic cord as a whip
- Pretending the mic is your penis (and/or talking gina)
- Breathing heavy into the mic, pretending you're Darth Vader

Sadly, advancements in technology are slowly edging this classic piece of shtick into the realm of "old school" (not the good kind). Take advantage while you can, but look to the future; remember what happened to the Megaphone Comedian.

WHERE YOU'VE SEEN IT BEFORE

See list of comedy clubs at back of book in your hand. Also, any emcee anywhere at anything. The classic mic catchphrase, "Is this on?" also works in bed when your penis stops working – you'll get the kind of sad laugh you're hoping for from your disappointed mate. (If you're a woman reading this, then try that line on any flaccid partner – a true test of whether or not this is "the one" is whether or not he can laugh at his own sexual failures).

#73 — MILITARY HI-JINX

"Private gung-ho," "Ensign fatty," "Corporal psycho," "Sergeant homo-phobe," "Lieutenant kiss-ass," and "General incompetent"... these are good foundation characters for a top-notch humor-in-uniform bit (allit-eration courtesy of *Reader's Digest* – thanks, *Reader's Digest*!). Cops unable to catch a thief can be a funny shtick. Please note: one cop running and falling is sad, two cops running and falling can be disheartening, but fifteen cops trying to catch a hobo and all running into the same light pole one after another is a hoot.

#74 — MIMES / PANTOMIME

A MIME is one who PANTOMIMES... easy to remember, right? Mimes had their heyday back in France during the 1940s. The French had all that free time that otherwise would have been used fighting the Nazis in WWII and they put their minds together to create a new art form based in silence (coincidence?). While pantomiming can be a new high (especially with some jaunty jazz fusion in the background), the job of miming itself is dead – as is making fun of mimes.... it needs a fresh twist, it's already been used with almost every other number. Will require new technology to be truly funny again.

We recommend that you try pantomiming at home or around the neighborhood in order to gauge reaction. Most likely, you'll get blank stares, but people will pick you for their charades team at a party! "Pantomime is the route to Popularity!"© pending

THINGS YOU CAN PRETEND YOU ARE TRAPPED IN TO SHOW OFF YOUR PANTOMIMING SKILLS

Box, jail cell, vagina, smaller box, space capsule, Happy Meal, a bur-rito as big as your head, back end of a unicorn costume, wind tunnel, time machine shaped like a vagina.

WHERE YOU'VE SEEN THIS BEFORE
- Urban streets
- France
- The '60s

ELEMENTS OF A SUCCESSFUL MIRROR ROUTINE

The fake-out.

The surprise attack.

EXTRA CREDIT:
DOUBLE YOUR LAUGH

Different hats.

Inadvertent Hitler mustache.

COMEDY FACT!

Loud-mouthed minister-turned-comedian
Sam Kinison, known for his screaming rants
and no-holds-barred opinions, wore a beret
and died in a drunk driving incident.

#75 — MIRROR ROUTINE

Good birthday gift for a fellow comedian. Made famous in a TV episode of *I Love Lucy* by Harpo Marx and Lucille Ball in their groundbreaking "Which one is a great comedian and which one coasted on the coattails of his funnier brothers?" routine.

KEYS TO THE VAN

That's really just a phrase, sorry. We were trying to be cute. Believe it or not, the important key to a good mirror routine is actually NOT having a mirror. Like with many things in life, it requires intense concentration, great listening, and full use of your body. You'll see by the intricate diagrams that you will be required to be able to coordinate your movements with another person. This is one of the few comedy numbers that has no practical purpose in life unless you seek to mock one of your foes, in which case they will be very upset to be "mirrored"!

#76 — MISPRONUNCIATION OF WORDS

This is different than a #7 (Big Words/Made-Up Words) in that the goal is to not challenge the audience's reference level by creating a word they never heard of – the challenge is to hilariously say words in the wrong way! Names, places and crucial plot information can be mangled beyond recognition. Norm Crosby© built a career out of this little gem of a bit and look where he is today!

HOW YOU CAN USE THIS IN YOUR REAL LIFE

Let's say you work in an office. Pick a word that you use every day – let's say the word "publicity." Which is perfect because actually you work in a Public Relations firm where you represent, publicly, some of the hot young stars of today (and tomorrow). For example: you often chauffeur around one of the Hilton sisters to their many appearances. This is a great job, but you sense that it could be soulless in some way. You start to think about livening up your life, and then you realize that what you really want to be is "funny"! Well, you're in the perfect business to apply this number AND get lots of laughs AND possibly an entrée into the world of comedy! In order to get laughs while you're doing your job, start to refer to your job as "Pubic Relations." By mispronouncing the word *public* as "pubic" (dropping the "L"), you've created an entirely different job description – and funny to boot, because *pubic* is one of the top 100 funny words ever! Yes, it sounds like "a line" and it sounds "stupid," but if you say it a lot at parties, and people laugh, then it might get back to some famous comedian and they could take you under their wing! Being under a comedian's wing should definitely be a goal in your "How I'm Going to Be a Success" diary!

WHERE YOU'VE SEEN THIS BEFORE
- Serge – *Beverly Hills Cop*
- Archie Bunker – *All in the Family*
- Martin Short's wedding-planner character – *Father of the Bride*
- Any US president during the early 2000s

SLIPPING ON A BANANA PEEL

RIGHT   **WRONG**

CREATING A UNIQUE CHARACTER

CASE STUDY: THE COMPLETE BOOB

The complete boob is an exciting character that NEVER goes out of style in the world of sketch comedy. Purchase these items ONCE and you're set for LIFE!

FROM TOP TO BOTTOM!!!

Comedy Hat: What you need is a good, soft fedora which can be molded to your specifications. The fit should be loose, but firm enough to withstand roughhousing. The brim must be pliable, yet sturdy when set. The boob wears his brim up.

Wig: Not absolutely essential (if your comedy hat is in order), but for the complete boob look, why not splurge and go for it and do it up and shoot the works?

Funny Glasses: This item is particularly boobish. Horn-rimmed and thick will get the job done. Real coke-bottle lenses a plus! Avoid your own real prescription for funny balance mishaps.

Fake Teeth: Makes saying "buhh" all the more believable.

Comedy Tie: The 1970s were the Golden Age for comedy ties. ('Course, they didn't know it at the time — guys were getting laid with this stuff!) And clip-ons only, please — don't embarrass yourself.

Comedy Jacket: Your boobery will be judged on the merit of your jacket. Is it patterned? And then patterned again? Does the sleeve ride up the arm? Are the lapels their widest? And that better not be linen I'm looking at! SNAP!

#77 — MISSING TEETH / SPACE BETWEEN TEETH

If you're born with this hilarious deformity, then it's God or Buddha demanding you be a comedian! Or a hillbilly! See Terry Thomas; David Letterman; any boxing sketch.

DON'T GIVE IN TO SOCIETAL PEER PRESSURE!

There are a lot of very funny looking 12-year-olds whose lives and potential comedy careers are ruined by peer pressure: the pressure to have normal, straight teeth. Instead of developing a lifelong character such as the "pretty-girl-from-the-back/ugly-bucktoothed-girl-from-the-front" part, parents seem determined to get their child orthodontic treatment. Braces can be funny SHORT-TERM, sure, but a messed-up mouth can be a LONG-TERM character trait! We HOPE that this book is being read and/or stolen and then read by 12-year-olds who might heed this warning, but if you're a parent with an oddly-toothed child, PLEASE, listen to us and let your child be gawked at – your banker will thank you!

TRY THIS AT HOME / OUTSIDE OF HOME

Take a black marker and cover one of your front teeth, so that you have a "temporary" gap tooth. Then take it out for a "comedy spin." Go out for dinner and see if you get a laugh from the waitress, go to a bar and see if the chicks laugh at your teeth, go to the gym and smile at a guy in the shower… you'll get a laugh anywhere with this deformity!

#78 — MISSPELLING IMPORTANT INFORMATION

For the literate comedian only! First you need to know how to spell, then you can wrench the laughs from "mis"spelling!

WHAT QUALIFIES AS "IMPORTANT INFORMATION"?

- Death Certificate
- Menu at the Final Supper
- Cable bill

REMEMBER THIS SCENE?

One of the highlights of Woody Allen's groundbreaking comedy of errors, *Take The Money and Run,* is a scene with a poorly written bank robber's note. Woody also married his stepdaughter.

HOW YOU CAN USE THIS IN YOUR REAL LIFE

Let's say you work in an office. Let's say that it's a big enough office to have an employee lunchroom with a bulletin board. This is an opportunity for you to put up funny notes about office policy or something. We recommend that you do it anonymously in order to gauge reaction amongst the staff before you step up to claim those notes as your own.

For example: In our scientific hypothetical, your boss's name is Charles Nuetbeige (possibly of Scandanavian origin) and you start putting up notes with light-hearted office rules and signing them, "This is to be the new office policy. C. Nutbag." IF your boss has a sense of humor, he'll allow those notes to stay on the board for a few days; IF he does that, we recommend you tell everyone that you were the employee who was clever enough to misspell the boss's name for comedic effect. If he doesn't appear to like the note, we suggest you not tell anyone that it was your big idea.

COMEDY FACT!

Of hilarious silent film comedian Harry Langdon, Frank Capra once said, "He was the most tragic figure I ever came across in show business."

#79 — MISTAKEN IDENTITY

Long-haired guys with great asses mistaken for hot chicks is just a primo example of this comedy cornerstone. Writers have used twins, foreigners, the pretentious, and those with short attention spans as inspiration for this source of yuks. For the comedy snobs who might read this, please note that Shakespeare DID NOT invent this device — besides, it hasn't even been proven that Shakespeare had arms.

LITTLE KNOWN FACT: This bit was worked on simultaneously by comedy scientists in Appleton, Wisconsin and pre-Stalin Russia.

HOW TO DO THIS AND GET LAUGHS IN YOUR VERY OWN HOME

Little kids love it when you tease them. If you have two children, call the boy by the girl's name and vice versa until they either laugh or scream. Insist that they are not who they think they are. Keep it up for as long as possible for maximum comedic/psychological effect.

HOW YOU CAN GET LAUGHS AND/OR A DATE OUTSIDE THE HOME

Try to go to the same diner every day. Get to know one of the waitresses there. If the diner you have chosen has unattractive waitresses, find another diner. Oh, we forgot — what would be BEST is if it was an attractive waitress with a nameplate on her uniform. Sorry about that. Okay; as you get more comfortable there, start to call her by a different name every day — she might or might not correct you — but either way, joking about the fact that you "forget" her name every day could become a bond between the two of you. Eventually she'll start to giggle and get excited thinking about what new name you'll call her each day… this story is almost writing itself. She'll think your memory game is cute and go out with you. That would be the ideal scenario.

WHERE YOU'VE SEEN THIS BEFORE
- Mel Brooks's *History of the World Part 1* (king/pauper)
- Tom Hanks's *Bachelor Party* (transvestite hooker)
- Eddie Murphy's career (transvestite hooker)

#80 — MR. CLUMSY

A good "laugh tester." Not to be confused with a general #100 (Physical/Shtick) action, a good clumsy character can be career defining. Once a character's innate clumsiness has been established, the audience will gleefully follow along wondering what kind of comedic trouble "Mr. Clumsy" will get into next! Good Examples: A classic "Mr. Clumsy" will be proficient at putting a hand on one end of a book shelf and having it collapse whereby all the books come crashing into him; or trying to gently set a piece of glass in a glass display case only to sneeze and destroy the entire cabinet of delicate objects. Ask yourself, would my comedy scene benefit by the intrusion of someone incapable of standing still?

LOCATION LOCATION LOCATION
You'll never miss getting a laugh by having MR. CLUMSY show up in these locations!

- Jelly Bean Factory
- Ball-Bearings Store
- Glass-Blowing Museum made of Glass
- Bris for Twins (RABBI Clumsy to you!)
- Cloning laboratory with huge signs that say "BE CAREFUL"

#81 — MR. KNOW-IT-ALL

One thing we've learned over the years is that people both love and hate the intelligentsia. Since most people are stupid, employing a "Mr. Know-It-All" character who supplies elaborative inventive answers to any question is a sure-fire way to capitalize on your audience's probable stupidity. We have great respect for both audiences and know-it-alls and sincerely hope that some day they can live in peace together. It will be tough, though, because putting one over on the audience is as old as old is.

#82 — MOVIE SPOOFS

Some people spend years of their lives, resources, energy, and all of their talent creating entertainment for others to enjoy. And not just any kind of entertainment. They search their souls and pour their hearts and passion into artistic statements, forcing humanity to look within itself for the answers to the burning questions of our time. Other people think it's hilarious to goof on those creations, and we're definitely in category 2! Once a classic movie is out there for all to see, it's your democratic right to get a laugh by giving that movie a porn title. Sure there's spoofs like *Spaceballs, Blazing Saddles,* and anything Weird Al ever created, but some of the best movie-title send-ups around can be found in the bawdy world of smut. There's a lot we can learn from sex.

CLASSIC MOVIE SPOOF TITLES (PORN)

- *Poke-a-cuntus*
- *Schindler's Fist*
- *The Pound of Music*
- *Blow-Up*
- *When Harry Felched Sally*
- *Paps*
- *The Midget Sex Version of To Kill a Mockingbird*

NON-PORN MOVIE-SPOOF SAMPLE DIALOGUE TO BE SHARED WITH THE CHILD THAT YOU'RE BUYING THIS BOOK FOR

- "The first rule of Polite Club – don't talk about Polite Club. Please."
- "I'm bald as hell and I'm not gonna take it anymore!"
- "You talkin' to pee?"
- "Forget it, Jake – it's Funkytown."
- "Ron Livingston, I presume."
- "I'm out of quarters? You're out of quarters! This entire courtroom is out of quarters!"
- "Luke, I'm your career." "Nooooooo!!"
- "Lorena Bobbitt, I think this is the beginning of a beautiful friendship."
- "Gattaca! Gattaca! Gattaca!"
- "Frankly, my dear, I don't give a fuck."

#83 — MUSICAL SPOOFS

Musicals are easy to spoof because they are so unnatural. Most people don't break out into song upon being asked "How are you this morning?" As a matter of fact, people who break into song frighten us. Spoofing them is our way of saying, "We're not going to take your damn singing!" It's what we call "defensive comedy" and it's been around since shortly after the first musical tortured us. Spoofmeisters such as Mel Brooks use their comedic skills to rid the world of its ills – sadly, sometimes comedy just needs world ills to exist. Think of it. Without the Nazis, Mel Brooks would never have won all those damn Tonys for *The Producers*. To their lasting chagrin, Mel didn't thank the Nazis during his acceptance speech.

HOW YOU CAN USE THIS IN YOUR REAL LIFE

Let's say it's the holidays. Let's also say that you have one of those karaoke machines (you got it for LAST Christmas), and by now you've gone through all the songs. It's just not the cool thing anymore… well, wait just one #83 second! Why not invite some friends over for a seemingly typical holiday party – egg nog, laughing about Jesus – and then break out your new "Parodoake Machine"! You can take ALL the songs from the machine and create exciting new versions for the amusement of others!

Make up new words to such seemingly boring hits as:

- "Yesterday" becomes "Today!"
- "Born to Run" becomes "Born for Fun!"
- "Let's Spend the Night Together" becomes "Let's Spend Some Time Together!"

Even if you can't sing, your ability to make fun of the creations of other more talented singer/songwriters will shine through and stamp you as "crazy" and "inventive." Yeah you.

#84 — NOT FUNNY AFTER REHAB

This is not so much a comedy bit as a comedy warning! If you're already a drinker, or meth head, or crack escort, then you're already halfway to being a successful comedian! Whereas in most professions this can be a road to downfall, in comedy - and this is proven – being high makes you <u>funnier</u>.

A WORD TO THE WISE

Wanna foolishly nip your sense of humor in the bud? Visit a therapist and find out "why" you're funny. Yes, the world is filled with those who would rob you of your talent for personal gain.

HOW TO REFER TO YOUR ALTERED STATE

So here are some cute ways to refer to your altered state and thereby soften the experience for everyone:

- "I'm a little in the suds."
- "I'm just whisky-frisky, that's all."
- "What, smoking glue isn't cool anymore?"

<u>COMICS NOT FUNNY AFTER REHAB</u>

All of them.

<u>COMICS' CAREERS STILL "ALIVE" AFTER REHAB</u>

None of them.

Leave your funny at the door.

#85 — NON SEQUITURS

Simply say something that has nothing to do with whatever the topic of conversation is. How easy is that!

EXAMPLES OF ACTUAL THINGS PEOPLE MIGHT SAY TO YOU:
- "Would you like fries with that?"
- "Do you know the time?"
- "Have you thought about your insurance needs?"
- "Oh, your baby is soooo cute!"

EXAMPLES OF NON-SEQUITUR REPLIES FOR YOU TO USE FREE OF CHARGE SINCE YOU PAID FOR THIS BOOK (*APPLY AS NEEDED*)
- "Pillows make delicious elephants."
- "Well, that's a bowl of hot nothing."
- "Spain is my new black."
- "Spare me the trigonometry."
- "Except for this mole on my chin, I'm simply not ready to be the president of your hair."
- "Let's go down the block and block that down."
- "My little sister's mule would give your nads a lickfest if you just paid the cashier with dreams."

WHERE YOU'VE SEEN IT BEFORE
Marx Brothers; Monty Python; *Goon Show*; Bush Administration; *Anna Nicole Smith Show.*

COMEDY FACT!

Caustic comedienne and shopping network magnate Joan Rivers berated her husband Edgar in her stand-up act. He later committed suicide.

#86 — NOVELTY ITEMS

The squirting flower, the whoopee cushion, the dribble glass, the phony dog poop, the nickel-nail. In the dark days before COMEDY BY THE NUMBERS,© the amateur joke-smith had to rely upon these Spencer's Gifts staples for his/her (mainly his) humor diet.

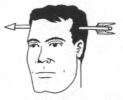

SOME NOVELTY ITEMS THAT NEVER CAUGHT ON

Itchy milk; exploding eye patch; shit gum; black-light HIV test; trick real machete; phantom-leg hot-foot; gassy nun's habit; jumbo toe; Hitler lipstick; razor-sharp crayon box; "You're Dead, Cocksucker"– inscribed pencils; firecracker teeth; syphilis-ink pen; creaky heart monitor; flaming-hot mouse trap; dirt-in-a-bottle; "stinky" drink coasters; phony rape-is-legal contract; placebo sun-tan lotion; "squirting" glass eye; hobo negligee; leaky-mercury anal thermometer; farting brick; measles underwear; asbestos wig; "We Had To Put Him To Sleep" balloon animal; bendy turd; mosquito-on-a-stick; "50 Things To Do With Your Dead Child" book; wee-wee toothpicks; bouncing ice cubes; never-light emergency flares; cat cock ring; indestructible ice cream; pills that make you vomit boxing gloves; prancing foot-odor moustache; fag soap; embarrassing tit condom; lice beer; faux insulin; jumbo eyelash; candy AIDS medicine; smiley-face x-ray; unbreakable fire alarm; poo-poo eye drops; sexy edible shoe insoles; shrinky toilet paper; invisible-ink "missing child" poster; President Anne Frank dollar bill; halitosis adult board game; "Suicide Scruffy" dog noose; whoopee IV bag; dead-relative Halloween mask; foot-ointment gum; "The 12 Stages Of Body Decay" playing cards; vomit bikini; decapitation-anniversary cards; "Keep On Truckin' " inscribed on the head of a pin; sad buzzer; prison Spanish fly; oversized dead Beatles checklist; singing oil-spill seagull; plastic-surgery Farrah Fawcett poster; "World's Greatest Grampa" coffin comforter; pet fingernail.

THE BATTLE OF THE CENTURY!
WHEN TWO TRIBES GO TO WAR!
The following comedy ad combines #29 (Doctored Photos)
with #86 (Novelty Items). Which number is funnier? YOU DECIDE!

#87 — NOVELTY RECORDS

"The Streak"; "The Energy Crisis of '72"; "My Bologna"; "Mr. Jaws"; "Kung Fu Fighting." The ditties that take advantage of fads, trends, and catchphrases are nothing less than an historical record of what's happening in our society at a given time — like lame time capsules. (**TOTALLY A FACT:** More people remember where they were when they first heard "Fish Heads" than knew where they were when Kennedy was sailing!) Yes, who among us <u>hasn't</u> dreamt of writing The Great American Novelty Record? Your humble authors have tried and failed. One thing we've learned for sure: just because people talk about AIDS a lot doesn't mean it's necessarily going to make a good novelty record.

WHAT YOU DON'T NEED TO USE THIS BIT
Any kind of musical talent.

#88 — OBJECT WORK

Digs into the very bowels of pretending. It's like a scene without props or a pantomime without dialogue. Start with making a sandwich, then move on to telephones and typewriters.

REMEMBER:
The First Rule of Drinking Tea is, and will always be, "Pinkies Up!" Subconsciously, an audience can't "accept" the invisible object without it.

For EXTRA FUN, try adding some exaggeration! <u>HERE'S HOW YOU DO IT:</u> If the object you're miming is normally small, make like it's larger-than-life (giant doorknob)! If the object is traditionally thought to be on the big side, why not make it next-to-miniscule (pee-wee sword)! Laughs will come running!

OTHER "OBJECT WORK" SIZE/WEIGHT-DISTORTION BITS
- Oddly shaped / mutt
- Light-as-a-feather / tubby guy
- Gigantic / roofing tack
- Super-heavy / shoe laces
- Teeny-weeny / moustache comb

FOR "BLUE" COMEDIANS ONLY

Object Work will come in "handy" with your Masturbation Routine. (Some of the "popular" guys like to throw in the "master debater" joke here as well; it's your call.) Personal Abuse shtick can be readily filed under "Cringe" Comedy (see elsewhere in this book), but has its roots in "Skool-yard Laffs" (to be covered in our sequel, God willing. Keep buying copies of this book!). But let's face it, what gets the whole bit going in the first place is what you're masturbating to. Grotesque public officials are always good, or you could slay 'em with the inappropriate (i.e., pleasuring yourself to the image of America's favorite humor dog, Marmaduke.) (Warning: Referencing Marmaduke may bring the house down.) Works well with Excuses (#32).

Okay, now YOU'RE ready to start using Object Work in YOUR home and YOUR workplace. Luckily, everything from a joke at the gym to a tall tale can benefit from a #88. Below is an everyday story you can use for training purposes. Don't be afraid. If you give up, you will never succeed.

TRAINING STORY

"So listen to this. This morning I woke up [*mime yawn*] and opened the front door [*mime opening door; also, creaking sound effect (#127)*]. I walked outside [*mime walking*] and picked a pretty dandelion [*size distortion: flower big as a mighty oak*]. You know, for my girlfriend. I picked a bunch of them [*multiple size distortions: hard to carry a bunch of oak trees*]. Which got me laughing about how Dolores eats a sandwich! You know how she's all... [*Mime eating sandwich + mimicry of a familiar (Dolores)*]. Well, I hate to admit it, but that got me thinking about Janet Reno [*mime masturbation + size distortion: penis the size of eyelash*]. Hey, so my dick is small. At least that fish I almost caught last summer was big. It was this [*size distortion: arm length-sized fish*] big. Welp! See you guys later! [*Real walking*]"

#89 — OLD SCHOOL

"That's old school, dude!" is a good phrase to exclaim at parties when someone says something you don't understand. Just remember to be humble – there were funny people before you who did stuff that the other old people of that era thought was funny at the time, but you might think is stupid now (Chaplin eating his shoe, for example).

WHERE YOU'VE SEEN IT BEFORE

Everything funny before last year is technically "old school" to you. The hit comedy movie *Old School,* starring Matt Walsh (as "Walsh") and others, was seen as groundbreaking in its reinvention of the #14 – Catchphrase ("earmuffs").

OLD SCHOOL COMEDIAN YOU MIGHT NEVER HAVE HEARD OF

Jocko Magillicutty – "the tornado of comedy." Jocko has been slayin' 'em in Reno, and nowhere else, for over 40 years. He's performed for six presidents...he's ENTERTAINED three. But seriously, all Jocko needs is a microphone, a loud sports coat, and a drummer for the rim shots. Here's a sampling of his act:
- A waiter came up to me at a restaurant and said, "What is your order, sir?" and I said "Hey I'm a primate, why do you ask?" Get it? – Like as in order, genus, species and all that junk.
- Liver and onions go together like terrible meat and worse vegetable. Know what I'm saying, liver-haters? Get it?

#90 — ONE-MAN SHOW

Some of the great patriots of American History dabbled in the "One-Man Show" genre. Ben Franklin broke new ground in his unimaginatively titled Revolutionary War–era one-man musical, *How I invented Electricity with a Kite and some String.* History doesn't give enough credit to Stonewall Jackson's double-entendre-filled one-man comedy of manners, *My South is Rising!* – an 1861 monologue that incited the Civil War. And, sadly, it seems like we rarely read anymore about the tour-de-farce show by ex-president Teddy Roosevelt, called *You's Don't Have To Call Me Teddy!,* in which he played every member of the Roosevelt clan at an uproarious Thanksgiving dinner.

Don't be intimidated by those that have come before you! Just remember, it's okay to believe that everything in your life is entertaining to others.

HOW YOU CAN YOU USE THIS IN YOUR REAL LIFE

Let's say you work in an office. We have no doubts that there are funny things that happen to you EVERY DAY in that office. And there are people in your office that are "real characters." Keep a diary of what people around you say and do, because that could all be part of your show one day. Call your diary a "One-Man Show Diary" to distinguish it from your other "Comedy Goal" diaries. (If you're a woman, call it a "One-Woman Show Diary" – seems obvious to say that, but we didn't want to take any chances.) Good material for your OMS diary includes: your family (everyone has one!), crazy friends, people you've dated, the guy in the lobby, a homeless family on your block, your grandfather with a lisp, your ex-wife (or ex-husband), your children, and the people inside your head. Take all those thoughts, write them down, and then start rehearsing. Don't worry about editing yourself, because, remember, if it's on YOUR PAGE it should be ON YOUR STAGE!

We suggest trying to make a lot of money at your "day" job in order to self-finance your one-man show, because then you don't have to listen to anyone's opinion!

PLEASE

If you decide to take the trek down the road towards your one-man-show destiny, for god's sake just don't refer to it as "Bogosianesque."

#91 — ONE-UPSMANSHIP

Unlimited number of characters involved in series of declarations in which each character contrives a rationalization of superiority over the previous character's declaration and/or abilities. Funnier than it sounds.

#92 — ONE-DOWNSMANSHIP

Opposite of #91; bragging in reverse, you might say.

CLASSIC SCENE THAT YOU SHOULD MEMORIZE WITH THREE OF YOUR FRIENDS: The "4 Yorkshire Men" sketch, by Monty Python.

CLASS IS IN SESSION!

The following classic scene is an example of the hilarity that you can reap from pain.

From the smash-hit play *The Idiotic Death of Two Fools* (which has been described as *Waiting for Godot* taken to its logical conclusion), please enjoy this brief yet acerbically funny scene between two slackers (Chuck and Phil) who are waiting on a very important person. Like most slackers, they're chatting about stuff from their youth – "the greatest era in American pop culture."

[*A loft cluttered with Monkees, Gilligan's Island, and 1960s "spy craze" toys & paraphernalia. And a single lava lamp. Phil is lounging on a ratty couch; Chuck is standing. They have just finished a conversation about the nature of man/mankind.*]

                    CHUCK
        Yeah, you might be right, Phil — Eve
        Plumb's replacement on the *Brady Bunch*
        specials <u>does</u> deserve a reassessment. But
        back to what I was saying earlier: I hate
        Halloween. Especially this one year where
        I had to wear a god-awful underwhelming
        Batman costume.

                    PHIL
        Halloween. I have nothing but bad memories
        of Halloween from my childhood. I remem-
        ber one year, when I was eight, my parents
        covered me with broken glass and sent me
        out trick-or-treating as a Suicide Jumper.

                    CHUCK
        Well, I got over the Batman thing. That
        wasn't the worst. Next year my mom sent me
        out as a Heavy Smoker. Try and dig up <u>that</u>
        outfit.

                    PHIL
        That's nothing. I remember one year my

parents gave me a color TV set, made me run down the block, and then they called the cops on me. My costume was "The Thief."

CHUCK

Yeah well, you were a special-needs kid, because the year after that my mom dressed me as "The Monster Who Couldn't Come Back Home."

PHIL

Well when did they take the silver spoon out of your mouth? Cuz the next year my parents gave me an enema and sent me out trick-or-treating as Mr. Shitty Pants. ...I didn't get a whole lotta Halloween candy that year.

CHUCK

Well. Someone was Daddy's little favorite. Year after that, my dad smeared lamb lard all over me, stuck a Kukla puppet up my ass, stripped me bare naked, and sent me out as the Invisible Man. I said, "Dad, you can still <u>see</u> me, can't ya?" (*deadpan*)..."No."

PHIL

So how did it feel to grow up as a prince? Because one Halloween — and I'll never forget this Halloween — my parents made me memorize the Constitution, shot me up with heroin, and sent me out trick-or-treating as Lenny Bruce.

CHUCK

Year after that my costume was just "Boy Who Wears One of His Dad's Ties." That scared exactly no one.

THE END

#93 — OY VEY! HUMOR

A Norwegian (Prof. Hoffman) explains: "*I know when I hear this phrase "oy vey," in a movie film, that I'm watching a _funny_ Jewish person. If a Jewisher doesn't say "oy vey," I know he's supposed to be a _serious_ Jewish. Like when they play all of the hide-and-seek in world war WW. When a Mexican has said the "ay caramba" it is only the same. So is this.*"

WHY THIS IS DIFFERENT THAN #63 (JEWS AND THEIR IDIOSYNCRACIES)

This is a classic subset of Jewish comedy which is quite often based in the reaction to traumatic experiences, i.e. dating a Catholic girl. If anything, this would qualify as an ethnic catchphrase that has been adopted by the non-semitic community. Laughs are plentiful whenever you hear this seminal phrase uttered by a non-Jew.

EXAMPLES OF CHARACTERS YOU CAN HAVE SAY "OY VEY" WITH GUARANTEED LAUGH RESULTS

- Put-upon Cowboy
- Unfocused Village Idiot
- The Pope
- Harried Executioner
- Toddler caught in dryer
- Border-guard trainee

#94 — PAIN / REACTION TO PAIN

Not to be used by the squeamish. Pain comedy has been done to death by all the greats: when Laurel hits Hardy with a ladder, we laugh; when Mo puts Curly's head into a wood vice that would normally crush a heavy timber post, we laugh. Every comedian worth his weight in laughs is half sadist, half masochist, and half goofball. Practice your facial expressions (#44) and the laughs will heighten as the pain does! In any partnership that explores pain it's good to have a "safe word." Ours is "Baby Finster."

The King of Pantomime Comedy!
And the inventor of the "Rubber Limb Gag"

RED SANDWICH'S
PAIN REACTIONS!

Red's unique brand of sentimental comedy is regularly convulsing audiences from the 1950s. Mr. Sandwich has always known that a good pain reaction is a killer segue into pathos (his bread and butter). Here's Red in his heyday doing the expressions that made him famous. Name the pain, and Red's got a face for it. So funny it hurts!

BRAT HAMMERING NAIL IN STOMACH.

FOOT CHOPPED OFF WHILE TRYING TO FLIRT.

INDIAN SHOT ARROW IN WINDPIPE.

DEAD WIFE'S AUTOPSY PHOTOS.

TIGER BITES GROIN.

TIGER BITES GROIN (VARIANT).

#95 — PATHOS a.k.a. CHAPLIN SYNDROME a.k.a. THE THIRD MASK

The dictionary describes pathos as "the quality in something which arouses pity, sorrow, sympathy, etc." The dictionary has been wrong before, but this one they nailed the shit out of.

IS PATHOS FOR YOU? If awards and industry-wide respect interest you – indeed, if you can "see yourself"© accepting the Oscar™ – then pathos is your bittersweet ticket. And make no mistake; as a "funny guy/girl" (as Hollywood will label you), pathos is your only hope to ever win an award for acting. But even without an award, you'll still be respected© for your effort. (Sorry about all the underlining.) (Sorry again.) E.g.: The Little Tramp, Freddy the Freeloader, the Poor Soul – award-winners none of them. But brave, complicated, "tear warriors"? Yes. The Jealous will recommend you save the drama for your mama – but if you ever want to be truly *remembered*, then now is surely the time to introduce the world to your lovable/deaf/mute/hobo/wino character: "Squirty."

Squirty.

PATHOS REQUIREMENTS

Orphans, dogs, or the deathly ill (preferably a mother with coughing fits).

THE ORIGINAL KINGS OF PATHOS

Jerry Lewis, Robin Williams, Lou Costello, Jackie Gleason, Red Skelton, Peter Sellers, Drew Carey, Sid Caesar, Stan Laurel, Benny Hill, Richard Pryor, Jerry Lewis, Jerry Lewis, Harry Langdon, Jim Belushi, Charlie Chaplin, Richard Nixon.

WHERE PATHOS WORKS AT HOME
- To get out of chores → eat your shoe like it's spaghetti
- To get your choice of which TV show to watch → become father figure to sad kid with dirty face and wearing tattered clothes and an adult-size driving cap
- To get away with murder → amble down the street into sunset AND give flower to blind girl

#96 — PEE-PEE JOKE

Look, we all pee. It's a necessary part of our biological functioning. If we DID NOT pee, then the urine stored up in our bodies would force us to explode. Not funny, right? So, since God thought we should expel smelly, salty (so we've heard) liquid from our body, he probably also thought we should make fun of it! By adding a few select pee pee (or wee wee) jokes to your repertoire, you're doing God's work.

CLASSIC SET-UP SCENE: BABY PEES WHILE BEING CHANGED

This bit puts any scene on auto funny. First get a baby and fill it with some liquid. Then go to change its diaper – but do it prematurely. While the diaper is spread out and the baby's genitalia is accessible, have the baby pee on the changer! If you use the right prop syringe held just out of camera range, you can get an extended pee-stream laugh – including the "Is he or isn't he finished peeing on me?" moment.

BEST CHARACTERS TO BE PEED ON
- Captain of Industry
- Jesus Christ
- Society Matron about to host a dinner party for Elie Weisel

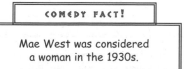

COMEDY FACT!

Mae West was considered a woman in the 1930s.

#97 — PEOPLE WHO SPEAK OUR LANGUAGE

Ironically, this number doesn't speak for itself. Here's a quick tip for you BEGINNERS — and it's only 2 EASY STEPS!

THE SET-UP

You're in a foreign land, where everyone you've been in contact with since arrival speaks nothing but mumbo-jumbo. You're ready to give up the idea of ever communicating with anyone in this mixed-up country. Because after all, you're only trying to find directions to the hotel! Finally, you approach someone who's obviously the village idiot. You now say this: "Do you... (*pointing at him*) you – know – know – (*pointing at your brain*) – know how to get to (*walking motion with fingers*) the Hotel (*mime sleeping*) Fabersham?"

THE PAY-OFF ("LAUGH")

This is when our foreign village idiot replies: "Yes. Take this road another five blocks until you see a broken-down melon cart. Directly across the street is the famous Hotel Fabersham. Indubitably. Uh, why are you looking at me like that? Is something the matter?" (You've just given him a #144 (The Double Take).)

#98 — PEOPLE WHO DON'T SPEAK OUR LANGUAGE

In the hilarious "McCarthy Era," there were those who thought that lothario Cuban lounge-singer Desi Arnaz was the leader of a Communist Plot to infiltrate our media (this was before the bongo was completely trusted). But from Dame Comedy's point of view, Desi was the template for funny foreigner/language jokes.

Requires a "normal" (i.e. English speaking) person to misunderstand.

COMEDY FACT!

Jim Belushi is the alive brother of funny dead man John Belushi.

#99 — PERSONAL THEME SONG

Here's how you can tell if a comedian is "on top of things" career-wise: watch them as they make an appearance on any late-night TV talk show; if the house band plays "Bad To The Bone" or "Walk This Way" during their entrance, then that comedian, clearly, is STUPID. And the same goes for YOU – there's no excuse for not having a memorable theme song! We apologize for the brusque tone, and it's the only time we'll use it, but a signature ditty is as important as a catchphrase and <u>twice</u> as important as your health.

>>>>**THIS <u>MIGHT</u> BE HELPFUL, BUT MAYBE NOT, DEPEND-ING ON YOU>>>>** If you're talented enough to be cast in a sitcom (and studies show all of you are), then that show's theme will invariably become yours, too! Problem (quickly) solved! (Not so with dramatic actors. To date, Ned Beatty has foolishly refused to use "Dueling Banjos" as a theme song.)

FAMOUS PERSONAL THEME SONGS
- Jackie Gleason / "Melancholy Serenade"
- The Three Stooges / "Three Blind Mice"
- Bob Hope / "Thanks For The Memories"
- Laurel and Hardy / "Waltz of the Cuckoos"
- Monty Python / "Liberty Bell March"
- Ernie Kovacs / "Oriental Blues"
- Groucho Marx / "Hooray For Capt. Spaulding"
- Dean Martin / "Everybody Loves Somebody Sometime"
- Bing Crosby / "White Christmas"
- Carol Burnett / "I'm So Glad We Had This Time Together"
- Bob Newhart / "Home To Emily"
- Eric Estrada / "Theme from *CHiPS*"
- Comedy By The Numbers / "Send in the Clowns (club remix)"

<u>SONGS STILL AVAILABLE FOR PERSONAL THEME SONGS</u>
The Cancer Song; The Messy Britches Overture; I Fuck Puppets Serenade; It's Not Easy Being a Wart; The Spinning Hubcap Song; I Am The Walrus (not the Beatles song); What A Day For A Love-in (by hippie rock band Capt. Spacefoot and the 3:00 Bananas & Cream Machine).

#100 — PHYSICAL COMEDY / SHTICK

Before there was sound, there was the pie.... before there was witti-ness, there was stepping on a rake.... before the put-down, there were two guys and a ladder.... NEVER BE AFRAID TO DO SHTICK. SOME PEOPLE JUST AREN'T THAT LUCKY!

HOW TO USE THIS IN YOUR REAL LIFE

Let's say you work in an office. It's the kind of office where you have to move a lot of boxes around. Okay, let's face it: it's a warehouse and your job is to move boxes around. If you want to both move boxes around all day AND get laughs, try to integrate some odd physical choices into your box-moving movements. For example: take a light box and when you bend down to pick it up pretend it's really really heavy! Wait for people to watch you as you lift, grunt, and strain until they think you're going to have a heart attack — then throw the box up in the air as if it were a box made of feathers. There are many examples of physical-comedy bits — so many, in fact, that our exam-ple almost feels inadequate. We're sorry.

PHYSICAL COMEDY AROUND THE WORLD

Although we all don't speak the same language, there is a great bond between cultures — we all laugh at physical comedy. Cannibals in the Amazon will howl at a snooty matron who slips and slides in the mud of their rainforest. It could be the same matron who slips on mud in Harlem while drug dealers on the corner laugh and the same matron character, yet again, who steps on camel shit and falls in the desert as members of the Taliban grab their stomachs in joy. What unites us is very often funnier than what divides us. (This could be seen as the take-away message from this book for all of you "important" reviewers who make it this far.)

COMEDY FACT!

Diminutive fun-ster David Spade is much taller than you might think.

#101 — PIE IN THE FACE

HALL OF FAME, CAN'T LOSE CATEGORY! One of the founding members of comedy. Before "talkies" were accidentally invented in pre-war New Jersey, characters displayed their disapproval of one another with shtick (#100), not the "f-ing" curses of today's comedians. Interestingly enough, the pie was originally designed to be a weapon, not the bakery staple that it is today. Imagine WWII fought today – with pies. The image of Pearl Harbor strewn with pie crust instead of mangled bodies could have been seen as a big gag instead of a tragic entry into a global conflict. Or the "Pie Raid on Entebbe." Whatever the violence – pies and shtick can often be the "healer."

In the interest of child safety, might we recommend the new Champro® Wiffle Cream Pie, for those little hands still in the formative stages of a sense of humor? Yes, nothing says "I care about you enough to prevent a possible accident with a timeless laugh-getting device" more than this exciting new addition to the world of Wiffle technology. Perfect for summer picnic season.

INTRODUCING A PIE IN A SCENE

The amazing thing about wringing a laugh out of this bit is that it's just as good if it occurs in a logically non-pie area. If you set up a scene in a pie factory, a pie in the face, or many pies in many faces, seems logical. BUT if you slam a pie into a face in a location where you wouldn't think there could possibly be pies, then you have heightened both the silliness of the scene and scored with the surprise factor!

EXAMPLES FOR USE OF PIES IN NON-PIE-LOGICAL LOCATIONS
- Confession booth
- Moon
- Gladiator fight

#102 — PLAYING DRUNK

Little-known fact: Foster Brooks portrayed a drunk for his entire career, but actually didn't start drinking until after he realized that this was the only thing he could do.

#103 — PLAYING MULTIPLE CHARACTERS

If this is your bag, then meet your new best friend: wigs (#168); your new associate: glasses (#49); more of an acquaintance: fake teeth (#49 also); your life partner: accents and dialects (next book, comedy-willing).

OKAY, we think we've been PRETTY CLEAR in this book that you really don't need any talent, or to be in any way original, to be funny and popular. This number is tricky though because, quite frankly, it would be better for you IF you HAD some talent. HOWEVER, we forge ahead under the original assumptions and hope you won't blame us if it doesn't work out that well.

HOW DO I USE THIS NUMBER IF I'M TRULY NOT TALENTED, LIKE YOU SUGGESTED IN THE ABOVE PARAGRAPH?

We love a challenge! There are some simple exercises that will enable you to discover your "character wheelhouse."© This is the phrase we invented to refer to the best characters you can do. Your safety zone. A lot of people think it's important to experiment and "stretch" yourself. We don't. If you are really good at stupid characters, then stick with it! If you can do a lisp and want to do a tugboat captain with a lisp, and a male nurse with a lisp, and a teaching assistant with a lisp (and maybe a sweater fetish) – then go for ith! Start by NOT WORRYING if you're doing a good job at your multiple characters! Don't stress.

First, think of 3 different jobs (like we did above)
Second, think of 3 different ages for your character
Third, imagine 3 different times of day
Fourth, imagine 3 different life-changing events (birth, death, loss of virginity, etc.)
Fifth, imagine 3 different locations

Okay, now create 3 different characters by mixing up the stuff above – it's a lot like the game "CLUE" (we get no royalties from that mention). Just ADD some other comedy numbers like #38, #52, #77, #144, and #159 until you get laughs. Let us know how it goes! The more characters you can do, the more you will be "respected"! (Which is a kissing cousin of "funny" and "popular.")

#103 ROYALTY: WATCH THESE COMEDY PRODUCTS TO SEE THE #103 IN ACTION!

- Carol Burnett: *The Carol Burnett Show*
- Lily Tomlin: *Laugh In*; her one-woman shows
- Tracey Ullman: *The Tracey Ullman Show*
- Sid Caesar: Y*our Show of Shows; Caesar's Hour; Little Me*
- Peter Sellers: *The Goon Show; The Mouse That Roared; Dr. Strangelove* (the ultimate #103 film!); *Soft Beds, Hard Battles* (six characters!); T*he Return of the Pink Panther; The Pink Panther Strikes Again; The Prisoner of Zenda*
- Dan Aykroyd: *Saturday Night Live; Dr. Detroit*
- Eddie Murphy: *Saturday Night Live; The Nutty Professor* films; *Coming To America;* his stand-up films
- Richard Pryor: *The Richard Pryor Show*; his stand-up films
- Jerry Lewis: *The Family Jewels*
- Alec Guinness: *Kind Hearts and Coronets* (eight characters!)

#104 — POLITICAL JOKES

Might seem similar to a #2 (Anti-Authoritarianism). To be truly "political" you should have an opinion-based punch line (Republicans ARE racists or Democrats ARE smarty pants) AND have enough integrity to change your opinion depending on the composition of your audiences. This bit combines well with the concept of hating someone. Fair warning: to some audiences, using a #104 is the same as saying "I read books" – which could equal career famine.

It is important to note that you do not need to have answers to the grave topics you touch on as you mock the leaders of our country – and others (is there a more hilarious target than Kaddahfi (sp?)?). The public expects that a real political comedian need only point out the faults of our "stars" for laughs, ridicule, and scorn in order to be popular and quoted.

FAMOUS POLITICAL JOKESTERS (WHITE GUYS ONLY)
Mort Sahl, Lenny Bruce, Johnny Carson, David Letterman, Jay Leno, Conan O'Brien, Jon Stewart, Stephen Colbert, Bill Maher, Dennis Miller (once)

FUNNIEST POLITICAL EVENT OF THE LAST 50 YEARS (TIE)
• Bill Clinton getting blowjob from Monica Lewinsky
• Bill Clinton getting blowjob from _____. (alleged)

WATERGATE – FUNNY OR NOT?
Scholars have debated just HOW funny the break-in at the Watergate Hotel in Washington by associates of the Republican National Committee and its subsequent cover-up by the Nixon White House was, but we have only one regret.

We wish that the break-in had happened at the John Hancock Hotel, JUST SO all future political scandals would have been named differently, i.e. Travelcock, Whitewatercock, etc.

COMEDY FACT!

Both funny AND gay comedienne Ellen DeGeneres famously announced her homosexuality on her groundbreaking sitcom. It was later cancelled.

#105 — POO POO JOKE

Look, we all make poo poo. It's a necessary part of our biological functioning. If we DID NOT make poo, then the waste stored up in our bodies would force us to explode. Not funny, right? So, since God thought we should expel smelly, salty (so we've heard) liquid/solids from our body, he probably also thought we should make fun of it! So, by adding a few select poo poo (or shit) jokes to your repertoire, you're doing God's work.

CLASSIC SET-UP SCENE: BABY SHITS WHILE BEING CHANGED

This bit puts any scene on auto funny. First get a baby and fill it with some liquid AND solids. Then go to change its diaper – but do it prematurely. While the diaper is spread out and the baby's genitalia is accessible, have the baby shit on the changer! If you use the right prop syringe held just out of camera range, you can get an extended baby shitstream laugh – including the "Is he or isn't he finished shitting on me?" moment.

BEST CHARACTERS TO BE SHAT ON
- Captain of Industry
- Supreme Court Justice
- Society Matron about to host a dinner party for Cindy Adams

#106 — PORTRAYING AN ANIMAL

Whether you're essaying the role of a dog, a chimp, or Godzilla, the only thing a smart audience will ever require of you is that you (a) dry hump the leg of a fellow performer, (b) play with/throw your own feces, and/or (c) smell a butt. Easy to do!

HOW DO I GET INTO THIS BIT ORGANICALLY?

Two words: hypnotism shtick.

HERE'S A SEXY DIVERSION!!!

On the road? Waiting in the green room for your headliner spot at the Comedy Store? Bored? We know how difficult it is to entertain an entertainer. Movies, magazines, amusement parks — nothing seems to be tailored specifically for the comedian on the go. Until now! How'dja like to curl up with a lusty, absorbing romance novel!? We proudly present the first page from Elizabeth R. Fontaine's *The Stallion* — a gothic tale of forbidden love and a young woman's sexual yearning for lust.

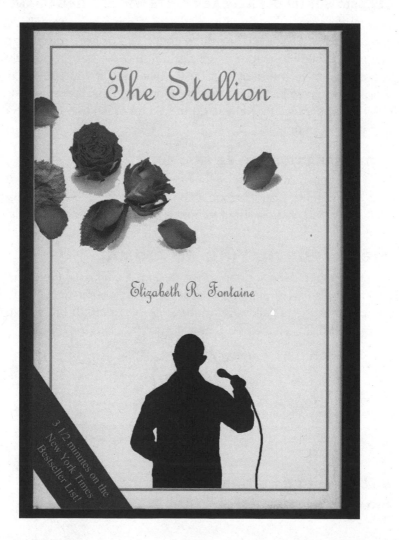

CHAPTER ONE

Tara laid on her Tudor waterbed, the crazy quilt not quite covering her smooth, naked, snow-white skin, and dreamt of Marco. Had it really only been a week since they'd first met? — at the open mic night at Knee-Slapperz in Cleveland? Yes, Costello! She reflected, it had only been a week — and yet it felt as if they had always known one another. Marco was a proud, dark-skinned Italian with long-flowing hair, muscular hands, clear, piercing eyes and a killer fart routine that had interested the bookers for Jimmy Kimmel. Just like her father. Oh, Marco, she thought, when will my neck be devoured again by the cruel, probing lips of The King of Farts?

Her thoughts wandered. What would her friends think of her love fore the brutal low comedian? They'd never understand the passion she felt for a boy from the wrong side of the tracks — a common gas comic. And what of Rex McKnight, her former lover and straight man? He would have plenty to say about Marco and how he'd once stolen a Monica Lewinsky joke from him on the eve of a Billy Crystal roast at the Friar's Club in New York. Rex would kill Marco, given the chance.

Tara fidgeted, her brow creasing like a familiar Sid Caesar facial expression. She decided to clear her mind of Rex and her friends and instead focus on her set that night at The Gut Buster on Third. Should she still lead with the Michael Jackson trial? The phone rang.

Tara padded to her cell phone, accidentally stepping on a whoopee cushion on the way (reminding her of Marco), and answered deliberately. "Hello? Tara speaking — live not Memorex."

"Tara, this is Jonathan." Jonathan Spanger was Tara's cutthroat, no-nonsense agent. He was a ruggedly handsome, silver-maned Lothario of a man — a seducer of some of the most beautiful women in the world — who'd made his fortune in *I Can't Believe I Ate The Whole Thing!* T-shirts in the 1970s.

"Oh, Jonathan." she said breathily, her chest heaving. "How's my favorite agent?"

Power oozed from his voice. "You know God damn well how I am. How long am I expected to continue with this insane charade? I'm sick of having to lie to everyone I know. You're performing at The Gut Buster tonight and I still don't have one single resume postcard of yours to flier the tables with?!? Is this how a stand-up treats a man on bended knee? A man who would gladly throw himself into the fiery guts of a volcano if he thought it would help you get your writing packet together for *Mad TV*?"

"I'm sorry, Jonathan. I — I totally spaced it." But her mind was elsewhere. On Marco, and their last passionate night together. He had kissed her lips gently after his "Famous Tooters Through History" bit and an encore. And she could hardly wait to explore the manly contours of his young, sweaty body as soon as she collected her cut from the night's door. In the back of Marco's Honda Accord, which had barely made it to Los Angeles from The Chuckle Hut in Pittsburgh, Tara and Marco had collapsed into one another's groping arms. Their hungry bodies intertwined, much like the riffing they'd enjoyed earlier regarding the erection of the President Clinton Library.

"I want you," Marco cracked. He slowly, almost dangerously, lowered his pants to reveal the *Objects Are Larger Than They Appear in Mirror* boxers he always wore for good luck.

"Yes!" she had screamed. "Yes and!"

#107 — PORTRAYING A DIFFERENT SEX

This one goes both ways! People generally laugh at their sexual inadequacies and are glad it's not them. Interestingly enough, not necessarily related to #106 (or so they say).

THE HISTORY OF PORTRAYING A DIFFERENT SEX

Started it all, as we know the bit today: *Some Like It Hot*
Brought it to television: Milton Berle
Revived it for a modern audience: Dustin Hoffman in *Tootsie*
Classic #107 user whom all modern #107 users mention during promotional junkets: William Shakespeare
Officially killed it: Bruce Vilanch in *Hairspray*

HOW YOU CAN USE THIS IN YOUR REAL LIFE

Let's say you work in an office. You're bored at your job as a paralegal for an international food-service conglomerate and are searching for a way to bring laughter into your workplace AND give yourself an excuse to shave your legs. This number is perfect for you. First, start asking your female associates where they shop (sorry, we just realized that this scenario will be strictly for a guy to use – women should just reverse everything they read. You're smart, you'll figure it out). Start leaving work a little early to do some shopping. If you want to start tongues awagging, then shop local! On the Friday before your big coming-out, tell everyone that your horoscope predicted big changes for you, but pretend not to know what that means! Then come in on Monday morning all dressed up like a whore. This will be so funny. We wish we were there.

#108 — PROP COMEDY

Frowned upon, yes. But insanely reliable. This sub-culture of comedians has its own language and ways. If you were to listen in on a conversation between Carrot Top and Gallagher, odds are you would have no idea what they were talking about.

PROP COMEDY 101

Find a dumpster. No matter where you live, there must be dumpsters. Take as much stupid stuff as you can. Take it home and spread it out on the floor and stare at it until an idea comes to you.

Remember: one man's toilet brush is another man's (Carrot Top's) Britney Spears halo.

FAMOUS CHARACTERS WITH PROPS
- Kojak: lolly
- Ed Asner in *Roots*: whip
- *The Matrix*'s Keanu Reeves: "I'm gonna kick your ass" gaze

#109 — PUPPETS

When you think about it, no, <u>really</u> think about it, the hand merely mimics the human head whilst draped in felt and yarn. Before investing, ask yourself: is your hand the "talented one" on your body? If your nose or your fat is funnier, head in that direction.

"Talking."

WILL I BE POPULAR IF I BECOME A PUPPETEER?

Impossibly, you will get so much tail, you won't know what do with it all.

Studies have shown that women fall hard for puppeteers because of their childhood associations with fantasy life. If you are able to get JUST the right "prince" character on your left arm, you're sure to get that MILF in the front row with the 5-year-old twins on your right arm! Oddly enough, marionetteteers are still seen as the nerds of the industry.

OKAY, I GET IT, I'LL BE POPULAR, BUT WHAT ABOUT FUNNY??

Other non-MILF studies have shown that puppets make the best cover for mocking superiors (#2), slamming political systems (#104), and even sex-joke telling (#120). You can have your puppet characters say things that *you* would only say in internet chat rooms – go for it! Puppets are your big chance to get laughs with material that's "not you"… which is perfect if "you" is "not funny"!

#110 — RACIAL HUMOR

Will label you either as "edgy" or "that racist motherfucker." Best when told to own kind.

RACIST WORDS THAT SOMETIMES ARE / AREN'T FUNNY
- The N-Word (African Americans)
- The C-Word (Chinese and all Asians)
- The K-Word (Jews)
- The S-Word (Hispanics)
- The other N-word (Germans, White Supremicists)

RACIAL HUMOR IN THE FUTURE

Here's a comedy heads-up: In the future, replicants will be derogatorily referred to as "skin jobs" and humans will be called "animals" by "damn dirty" apes. The future will thought-provokingly destroy comedy.

HOW YOU CAN USE THIS IN YOUR REAL LIFE

You really shouldn't. Save the racial comedy for films and stage shows where your hate can be masked by the specter of "creativity."

comedy classics collector's stamps
CLIP 'EM AND COLLECT 'EM!

THE CIGAR SERIES A 2

FUNNY HAIR SERIES A 15

ABUSE SERIES A 19

WARNING: Licking stamp may cause explosive diarrhea.

#111 — REFERENCING A SITCOM CHARACTER

Easy way to both curry favor with an audience and also to determine their threshold for laughter... good to test waters with "na nu, na nu." We have a theory that audiences like to be comfortable. They don't want to be challenged with new or original thought as much as they'd like to hear you mention ALF. They know ALF, they trust ALF, they will laugh at ALF's antics and commentary on the American Family. If you're on stage and can do an impression of ALF, then by god, you're going to kill. People will think you're cool because you watch the same TV show as them!

HOW CAN I CREATE A SITCOM CHARACTER THAT WILL BE AT AN "ALF-RECOGNIZABLE" LEVEL?

It's tough, we'll be honest. You can shoot for your ALFs, your Morks, your Urkels, your Fonzies, your Squiggys, your Kramers, your Jennifer Anistons – but you really have to catch lightning in a bottle to create a character that is THAT loveable right away. We suggest starting with an ethnic alien of some kind and working your way up. Try out the character on friends at lunch – possibly as a #109 (Puppet) – and see what happens. We've been quite successful at creating sitcom characters, but our secret process is too potentially lucrative to give away; we're still deciding whether or not we should tell you exactly how to create a hit sitcom character in the sequel. For now, stick to referencing them to people around the water cooler and you'll be known as the Pop Culture Funny Guy in the office!

AUTHOR'S NOTE

We realize that you are probably wondering exactly which successful sitcom characters we've created. We would love to tell you, but unfortunately, protracted litigation forbids us from revealing that information. But check out Animal Planet in 2009 – we're gonna OWN the comedy on the station!

#112 — RELIGION

<u>Comedy of the Weird:</u> People who are religious **don't actually like religious humor!**

All organized groups (in this case, religious sects around the world) are potentially "humor targets," because they take themselves so darn seriously. We highly recommend making fun of religion, religious icons, religious theories, any/all commandments, seemingly real religions, etc., because it's one of the best opportunities for your comedy to affect the most people. By "affect," we mean "piss off."

This number is directly related to #2 (Anti-Authoritarianism). However, you have a lot more Jesus stuff to use with a #112.

Below is a handy reference list for all the major religions showing some of their "quirky" traits that you can exploit in your comedy. If you're lucky, your comedy will provoke a boycott from a specific religion.

> CATHOLICISM: Big on Jesus, uptight about sex, priests like little boys, other priests like little girls, nuns, lots of rules, the Pope is usually really old

> JUDAISM: Not so big on Jesus, lots of rules, some of them dress funny, blind faith in circumcision, rabbis with long beards

> MUSLIM: Big on Mohammed, like to rally, do not like to be made fun of, not so big on women having rights, all look the same to everyone else, highest percentage of martyrs

> SCIENTOLOGISTS: Big on Tom Cruise, not a real religion (maybe), mysterious rituals, well-manicured headquarters

> PROTESTANTS, EPISCOPALIANS, METHODISTS, BAPTISTS, ETC.: Indistinguishable from Catholics by non-Jesus-liking peoples

PYTHON VS. GOD

> *Monty Python's Life of Brian* — they "sum up all of religion in two minutes" with a scene where people follow Brian because of his sandal.

> *Monty Python's Meaning of Life* — they blame the world's overpopulation on Catholicism's hatred of birth control with their "Every Sperm is Sacred" toe-tapper.

> *Monty Python and the Holy Grail* — they have a castle full of virgins who want to be spanked (okay, not too satiric of religion, but it's virgins being spanked for God's sake!).

#113 — RETARDS / MENTALLY CHALLENGED

We'll be the first to sign a petition saying this is not an appropriate comedic bit or character stereotype. However, we'll also be the first to laugh at one! But that's us. This politically incorrect archetypal comedy staple is of course related to more numbers than any other and has been around since before the war of 1812 (known as "The War of the Retards" in certain circles). The psychological explanation is that the average person wants to see someone of limited mental capacity acting in an idiotic manner — this greatly enhances the viewer's self-esteem, thus leaving them more susceptible to laughing. It makes us feel better about ourselves to see a moron peeing into his pants or putting dirt in his/her hair — our own problems seem trivial. Besides, they also talk funny, face it.

(Sorry retards, we <u>have</u> to do this...)

FAMOUS COMEDY RETARDS
(WE'LL ALSO ACCEPT "SLOW PEOPLE")

Crazy "Craze" Guggenheim; The Scarecrow; Gomer Pyle; Ed Norton; Stan Laurel; Chauncey Gardner; Python's Gumby; Eccles; The Ringer; Junior Samples; Carl Spackler; The Jersey Guy; Steven Wright (all we're saying is, take the smart things he says out of the equation and he would sound like a <u>very</u> retarded individual); Goofy; Adam Sandler; Harpo; Ernest; The townsfolk in *Green Acres*; Navin Johnson; Kovacs' Eugene; Homer Simpson; Curly; Lou Costello; Most cartoon characters after being hit on the head; Inspector Clouseau; Jerry Lewis; Kramer; Pete Puma; Tracy Morgan; any Hobbitt; Gilligan; Joe Besser; Urkel; Balki; Latke; Jaws in *Moonraker*; Howard Borden; Dumb and Dumber <u>and</u> Dumberer; Frederick; The Weeb; Leonard; Charlie; Fredo Corleone.

COMEDY FACT!

The Canadian comedy troupe called Kids in the Hall once attempted American show business careers.

#114 — ROMANTIC COMEDY

Also called a "chick flick." Or a "bra bore-er," a "sexy snoozer," a "lip-stick loser," a "filly film," a "feel reel," a "broad baddie," a "Hugh Grant groaner." Coordinates well with many other numbers.

Take a girl to one of these and you've succeeded in using the Most Important Comedy Dating Tip Of Them All! You see? That FREE is already paying off!

WHERE YOU'VE SEEN IT BEFORE

If you've never dated a woman, you've <u>never</u> seen it.

HOW TO USE THIS IN YOUR REAL LIFE

Let's say you work in an office. The office, even if it's the long-haul trucker dispatch office you work in, is a perfect place for a lovey-dovey romantic comedy. Lots of fancy books will tell you to "write what you know," and who are we to disagree? Get your romantic story <u>from your own life.</u> We suggest, as a writing experiment, trying to romance one of your coworkers, all the while taking notes on the hilarious moments in your new relationship. You don't want to REALLY fall in love, because that could make you lose focus and damage your script, so you'll have to use "good judgment" as you pull this off. First, pick out a single woman in your office who appears to be lonely because she "can't find a good man." Actively ignore her, so that she has no idea that you're even pretending to be interested in her. Then, start with the gifts:

1. Get in early and leave a rose on her desk, but don't tell her it's from you.
2. Ask a neighbor if you can get their 4-year-old to draw lots of finger paintings of her and then leave them on her desk.
3. Get her a "panty of the month" membership and have it shipped to the office.
4. Leave a gift certificate to the "Babes in Toyland" Adult Sex Toy shop on her desk, with an anonymous note saying that "you" thought she needed to treat herself to a "pocket rocket."
5. Make a homemade card for her with cut-out letters from magazines.
6. Paint her car mauve and leave her a note (again anonymously) that says "You're too beautiful to have a regular color."

7. Stop by her desk once in a while and remark coyly on the gifts. She'll probably think that she's being wooed by someone else (let's say the handsome guy in the office), and you'll play along as if you're not interested (you're really not). AND THEN, just as she's about to get her self-esteem together and go over to speak to the office stud, drop the bomb on her that YOU were the one who gave her all the gifts as a gesture of your love for her! Here's where it gets tricky. What SHOULD happen is that she tells the boss on you and threatens a sexual-harassment suit. BUT, in your #114 movie story, her eyes widen, the music swells, and she laughs, as if to say, "You're my soul mate and I didn't even realize it!"

If she "gets" it, then she won't feel so bad when you tell her that you're not really interested. She'll love that she really "helped" your screenplay idea. She'll probably laugh and laugh and laugh. Probably.

#115 — RUBBER LEGS / LIMBS

Playing drunk (#102) is the primary benefactor of this number. (Chaucer had a rubber-leg act that killed. "The Canterbury Wails!" –The Times.)

HELPFUL HISTORY LESSON: Pretending that you have a leg made of rubber that prevents you from walking normally was a staple of Renaissance humor. Rubber-legged comedians were celebrated at the court of noted patrons the Medicis. Shortly after the Italians invented rubber, they began to create prosthetic limbs for the victims of the Crusades or some other religious war. Unfortunately, they created a nation of wobbly-armed and -legged ex-soldiers who had to turn to traveling circuses for their livelihood! This was quite the scandal for a long time – until a local Venetian comedy troupe began performing comedic skits with the heretofore-unappealing limbs. They became wildly popular. Word spread, and all of a sudden even able-bodied Italianos were cutting off their arms in order to get the "armos histericos" (funny arms) installed. Right up until WW I, the Italians led the charge, as such, in letting people know that this comedic device was "alrighta" with them!

Want to be the new Martin and Lewis? Study the work of Gene Spicey and Marty Jerome, "the comedy team that hates each other." Spicey was the perfect straight man, an alcoholic who only sang drinking songs. And Marty Jerome was always "on." I mean **always**. It was freaky. In the 1940s they regaled the country with humor movies like *Hey! We're in the Army!* and *Hi Hitler!* Their most famous bit was undoubtedly the classic "drill routine" from the film *Hold Those Privates!* Ready for some "dress-right-**mess**"?

"THE DRILL ROUTINE"

(Drill Sergeant Spicey marches Private Jerome onstage, calling cadence.)

SPICEY: Your momma was home when you left!

JEROME: You're right!

SPICEY: Your daddy was home when you left!

JEROME: You're right!

SPICEY: Detail… halt! Riiight face!

(Jerome does nothing.)

SPICEY: Marty, I said right face!

(Jerome finally sits on the ground.)

SPICEY: I said right face, you crum! Why'd you sit down?!

JEROME: (*child-like*) Oohhh, I don't know which direction "right" is! I'm just a little boy — three years old!

SPICEY: "Three!" Cut it out! Why do you always have to be so embarrassing? Stand up!

(Jerome stands up.)

SPICEY: Ah! I see you know which direction "up" is!

JEROME: I overheard some boys on the playground talkin' about up. **I** don't know what it is, though. I'm so young! Whooo!

SPICEY: Act sensible! You're thirty-eight! **Jesus** — you're thirty-eight! Shut up! Pre-sent **arms**!

JEROME: Okay, but I only got **one**. (He hands Spicey a plastic arm.)

SPICEY: (*enraged*) You **knew** I was going to eventually say that! That's why you were carrying around that phony arm all day!

JEROME: (*sings*) "Banana cream is loverly!"

Marty "on fire"

SPICEY: Will you stop thinking about pies! Now pipe down!

(Jerome sits down.)

SPICEY: Not "sit down!"

JEROME: I **am** sittin' down!

SPICEY: No, "pipe down!" Shut up! Okay, on your feet!

JEROME: I **am** on my feet! I'm **sittin'** on 'em!

SPICEY: Rrr. How the hell did you pass school?

JEROME: Easy. I walked right by it! Wowee!

SPICEY: No one in the world takes things as literally as you! You think it's **so** funny! You misunderstand everything! *(weakly)* Look, why don't you take it on the heel? I need to rehearse my big number for the USO show.

JEROME: Wellll… you promise you won't perform it without me?

SPICEY: I promise I — **no** I don't promise! This is a **solo** number!

JEROME: But I get to sing your song.

SPICEY: Yes — **NO!** Why do you always act like you can't hear me? It's incredibly bothersome! Now go! *(Jerome walks off with a mischievous smile.)* What an irritant. Okay, now I can

rehearse this song. It's called "On A Moon Like This" by Jean Cables. *(sings)* "On a moon like this I bought you a drink of boooooooze. Etc."

(During the song, Jerome re-enters and tries to drive Spicey insane. He hammers his feet with a real mallet; cuts his suit to ribbons with giant scissors; draws on his face with lipstick; individually plucks 20 hairs from his scalp; and finally, shoots him in the leg with a real pistol.)

(Spicey can take no more — they go at one another like rabid ostriches, kicking and screaming. Stage hands pull the boys apart.)

JEROME: Gene, you know why I hurt you? Cuz it's **funny!** SMOOCH! *(He kisses Spicey and they go at each other. Again the stage hands pull them apart.)*

STAGE HAND: *(Grabs Jerome by his lapels.)* Marty! You guys are the greatest comedy team there ever was — how can you do this to Spicey?

(The camera moves in on Jerome's face. As if to apologize for his actions, Jerome caps the scene with his catch phrase set to music.)

JEROME: *(sings)* "…I'm a mean widdle boy!"

Black out.

Not a publicity photo

#116 — SARCASM

If comedy were a coin, this would be the bitter "tail" side. Good in any situation where you need to defuse tension, e.g., AIDS research, murder trials, bat mitzvahs, gang jumps, hostage negotiations.

HOW YOU CAN USE THIS IN YOUR EVERYDAY LIFE

Let's say you work in an office. On a sitcom. Well, sarcasm will be used to comedic effect in everything you say. Try to practice with phrases such as "in your dreams" or "I bet." Also remember that most of the time you'll be using sarcasm to mask any sexual inadequacies that you have. Often confused with a cry for help or being an asshole.

#117 — SCARE COMEDY

As this can be a tricky number to accomplish correctly (the balance of frights and crackups must be impeccable), we thought it best to provide a helpful list of do's and don'ts for the home scare comedian and the coddled studio hack writing the *Van Helsing* sequel alike:

- **–DO** incorporate lots of blood.
- **–DO** use fake knives, skewers, machetes, cars, javelins, croquet mallets, garden claws, boiling water.
- **–DO** have lots of blood. Tons of it.
- **–DO** include a character that's afraid at some point.
- **–DO,** even if Dracula's not in your project, show all kinds of bloody blood. (Couldn't you put Dracula in just a little?)
- **–DO** not forget the blood.
- **–DON'T** make the Mummy do a triple take.
- **–DON'T** cast your child as Frankenstein.
- **–DON'T** use the word "boo."
- **–DON'T** show zombies brushing their teeth, shining their shoes, wig shopping, etc.
- **–DON'T** have Godzilla dance to "Let It Be" or "I'm Every Woman."

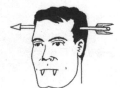

#118 — SCHOOLYARD LAFFS & TAUNTS

Farting; belching; grab-ass; humor with food stuffs; pull my finger – if your comedy isn't already tailored for children, you may never "make it" in this business. The reason? The public prefers their comedy wrapped in a man-child. If four out of five kids currently laugh at your material, you don't need this book.

WHERE YOU'VE SEEN IT BEFORE

Any schoolyard.

ALRIGHT, WE GIVE IN... HERE ARE SOME GOOD TAUNTS FOR YOU TO USE IN GETTING YOUR KICKS MOCKING SCHOOL KIDS (ALL OF THESE SHOULD BE SHOUTED)

- "Hey, fatty-fat-fat, have they weight-tested those swings?"
- "Hey girly, are those pebbles in your sweater or are you starting to grow breasts?"
- "Hey beanpole, can you reach that bird's ass for me?"
- "Hey, gayboy, are you a gayboy or what?"
- "Hey, I farted and your mother came out!"
- "Hey, doodyhead, stop picking your boogers and wiping them on your boner!" (homage to #9)

COMEDY FACT!

Acerbic comedienne Paula Poundstone was arrested for allegedly drinking around children.

#119 — SELF-DEPRECATION

The easy thing is to make fun of others (#68). But, the audience will love you for your honesty if you make fun of yourself first. Things about yourself to pick on include: your weight; your inability to get a date (probably because of your weight); how your parents have ruined you; how your kids are either ugly, stupid, greedy, or have stretched out your vagina and your breasts beyond recognition; your height; your inability to get a job (possibly because of your height); your wholly inadequate sex life; etc.

FACTS

4 out of 3 fat comedians will base their entire act on being fat – so if you're looking for easy material, start eating! If you're a woman, it's a piece of cake. If you're a fat woman, you should already have a date... with an agent!

KING OF SELF-DEP

Rodney Dangerfield, may he rest in peace, never let a night go by where he didn't essentially call himself an asshole. Maybe it was therapy.

REMEMBER: Self-deprecation and self-hate are two sides of the same mattress!

COMEDY JACKET

#120 — SEX JOKE

Look, we all have sex. It's a necessary part of our biological functioning. If we DID NOT have sex, then the juices stored up in our bodies would force us to explode. Not funny, right? So, since God thought we should expel smelly, salty (so we've heard) liquid/solids from our body, he probably also thought we should make fun of it! So, by adding a few select sex jokes to your repertoire, you're doing God's work.

WITH "SEX-JOKE TELLING," IT'S NOT SO MUCH "WHAT" THE JOKE IS, BUT "WHO'S" TELLING IT

Average types of folks will get laughs for even corny old sex jokes. If you NEED to get an R rating, then introduce one of these characters AND some shots of shaved beaver.

- Very old woman talking to her "girlfriends" at the home
- Hefty maids who don't speak English (it's okay to tell dirty jokes in foreign tongues)
- Lusty sharecropper
- Spinster aunt who lives in attic
- Iranian cab driver
- Your boss's daughter on "Take your Daughter to Work" Day

COMEDY TIE

#121 — SKETCHES / SKITS

<u>Comedy of the Weird:</u> Most comics will become insulted if you refer to their sketch as a skit – **even though the two words have the exact same meaning!**

One of the goals in your "important comedy goals" diary should be to write a comedy sketch/skit, get it produced and directed by local actors, and then sit back and wait for your sitcom break. This is the most common route to success.

COMMON SKETCH / SKIT LOCATIONS

- TV talk show of some kind
- School of some kind
- Bathroom of some kind
- Baseball ballpark somewhere
- Spain

HOW YOU CAN USE THIS IN YOUR REAL LIFE

Let's say you work in an office. It's the corporate headquarters of a national-brand kosher-hot-dog company. They make buns too. You have a funny idea that you've told the guys about at lunch – "What if our boss was a monkey?" Everyone cracks up. This is usually when most ideas die – at lunch – but you're determined to actually do something about it. One guy, Steve, says you should bring in an actual monkey and put him in Mr. Schwartz's office. Another guy, Mark, has a cousin who works for NBC and believes that this cousin could pass your idea along to the guys at *Saturday Night Live,* who he thinks would love it. The last guy in your posse, Marc (with a "c"), suggests that you take a writing course at the Discovery Center and expand on your sketch idea with the aid of a professional writing teacher. You consider all of those and then pick your own – you'll write a "sketch or skit" and put it on at the annual company talent show! If that goes well, you'll have a sense of accomplishment *and* you'll become popular as the guy who wrote that "hilarious monkey" sketch from the office show! Win win!

You work hard every day after work and finally come up with what you think is a "killer" sketch. You ask Steve, Mark, Marc, and Heather from the Casing Division to be in your sketch, which you've titled "Who's the Monkey?" It goes really well at the talent show, but your comedy piece loses out to Shelly Bletch's Israeli/Gospel folk song,

"L'Chaim Getting Married in the Morning." Sure you're disappointed, but you should realize that writing a sketch is all about the journey.

HINT!
Hollywood types LOVE IT when you format your creative work to conform with everyone else's creative work – otherwise they won't look at it.

#122 — SLAPPING

Can one possibly imagine a world of mirth without slapping? Although rarely used today, in its heyday 'twas a comedic staple. Imagine being Lou Costello in the 1940s: Because of an ever-increasing hatred you share with your partner, every time you say "How can a 'mudder' be a father?" you receive a crack to the face that makes even the union guys wince. Comedy as gold pieces!

SITUATIONS WHERE YOUR SLAP WILL GET YOU LAUGHS AND NOT ARRESTED
- Have a "fake" fight with your girlfriend at a pet store – then explain to the staff that you're just "pretend" fighting to see how the fishes react.
- You and your best friend get dressed up like Star Wars Storm Troopers and have a slap fight in an urban park. Crowds will gather just to watch with their own eyes!
- Become the inspecting officer for an Army platoon, then walk down a row of slightly disheveled trainees, slapping each face as you go by in succession (the most famous #122).

WHY DO I NEED TO KNOW THIS?
COMEDY BY THE NUMBERS© is looking to clarify, for the world, that violence, even in these most crucial of times, is integral to comedy. A lot of people put "sex" and "violence" together, which is true – BUT we contend that "violence" and "funny" should become more popular (although it's not a contest). If you can get down the well-placed, well-timed slap, then your comic arsenal just got a little bit bigger!

WOULD THE THREE STOOGES HAVE EXISTED WITHOUT THE INVENTION OF THE SLAP?
No.

#123 — SLOW-MOTION FIGHTING

Always a funny resolution to a "relationship" scene. The comedic value is heightened by #113s, #36s, and the use of the clergy.

HOW TO FIGHT IN SLOW MOTION

Some people think it's just taking a regular fight and slowing it down. While that's possible, we recommend the following "tricks of the slow-motion fighting trade."

- Remember your face is fighting too! Over-accentuate your facial expressions during any SMF.
- Introduce an action that the audience wouldn't normally see during a RSF (Regular-Speed Fight). For example, in the middle of throwing a punch, take a moment to notarize a piece of paper, then continue the punch.
- Let your limbs linger! A good SMF includes the "punch (and/or kick) that seems to take FOREVER to land." Your audience will drip with anticipation of the actual impact.
- Overreact to any touch. Let the whole body flail about from a mere tap – kids love it!

TIMING IS EVERYTHING

IMPORTANT! People are smart and will "get" the SMF PRETTY QUICKLY, so don't let it go on TOO long!

#124 — SOMEONE WHERE THEY DON'T WANT TO BE

Again, a comedy exercise that can involve something as simple as an abortion clinic or as complicated as an Army draft-induction cavity search. Just picture someone where they want to be and then create the opposite.

HOW YOU CAN USE THIS IN YOUR REAL LIFE

Let's say you work in an office. You've been selected to go to the big industry convention in Las Vegas. You're psyched because you've never been to Vegas, and you can't wait to have stories that you can't tell anyone about! So, after settling into your suite at Circus, Circus, you head out into the warm glow of the neon lights. But you drink a little too much and then you, for some reason, proposition a cop to have sex with you. Not an undercover cop, mind you, but a full-uniform-wearing, standing-in-front-of-the-precinct police officer. You ask him/her for sex. Cut to the next scene, and there you are (assuming you're white, right?) sitting in a jail cell. As the camera pulls back, we see that you're surrounded by a lot of typical jailees (blacks, probably, right?). One of them leans over your shoulder and says into the side of your scared face, "You're going to be my new pasty beey-otch!" People will enjoy the hilarious uncomfortableness of that situation (since it's not them). The laughter is directly related to a #110 (Racial Humor) and a partial #117 (Scare Comedy).

#125 — SOMEONE WHERE THEY SHOULDN'T BE

Lucille Ball owned the rights to this bit during the '50s and '60s, but according to legend sold it for a carton of smokes to famed director Alfred Hitchcock, who left it on a hooker's nightstand in lieu of payment. Lucy, as she was known then, was constantly going to places where Ricky didn't want her to go, but she couldn't help herself – and because of her psychological condition of ultra-curiosity mixed with an innate clumsiness, we as a nation laughed. The inappropriateness of it all is what gets us laughing.

TRY THIS EXERCISE

Get dressed up as a nun – with one of those "Flying Nun" habits, not the regular nun outfit – and then go into a strip club with a lot of single dollar bills.

THE REACTION?

Guaranteed weird looks as you stuff singles in the girls' G-strings – but you'll get residual laughs for days!

REMEMBER

Weird looks or groans = High-larity.©

TIP!

How to behave like a comedy scholar!

It has been said that "no one likes a know-it-all."
Whatever idiot said that probably wasn't funny. For
the comedy career-minded, the formula for success
must include having an encyclopedic knowledge of all
things humorous, why something is funny... and most
importantly, acting like you know all of this in front
of other people. For what good is knowing something
if no one knows you know it? Capiche? The highly-
regarded "Comedy Scholar" can be employed in a wide
variety of professions: head writer, executive producer, show creator, guru — the list literally goes
on and on.

   And you can be a Comedy Scholar in your everyday
life, too! Follow these easy-to-interpret instruc-
tions and soon your friends will be instantly looking
to you for a judgment on whether something is funny
or not. Here's how you do it:

1) First, memorize the entire contents of
   this book.

2) Then watch all of the movies and TV shows
   this book mentions as examples. You'll need
   to be ready to recite entire passages in
   order to prove your point to someone.

3) While watching a comedy on TV with your
   friends, mutter and nod at the jokes while
   saying things like: "That was good"; "Nice";
   "(sigh) They went too far"; and finally
   "Yeah, there were a few laughs in that."

By the way, all new students should select a performer, TV show, or movie, which you can claim
"invented it all." E.g., "You know, Sid Caesar practically invented the television sketch show." Then
try it out on a family member. Tell them everything
you know about *Your Show of Shows*. People love to
hear it! They want more talking talking talking! You
see, **Fun Facts + 'tude = Comedy Scholar.**

#126 — SONG PARODY

"I'd Like To Teach the World To Pee," or "The Sounds of Sirens," or "The Night Chicago Lied." Sure, this is related to a #83 (Musical Spoof), and there's a fine line between "parody" and "spoof," but by separating them into different numbers, we think we're highlighting the difference.

AND THE BIT GOES ON

It Was Just My Flatulation; I Wanna Hold Your Gland; Don't Fear the Reeker; Twist and Gout; Hey Prude; Rock You Like the Novocain; Black In Back; Porn In the USA; (And She's Buying a) Stairmaster To Heaven; Fear of a White Planet; Fatman; Blowing Me, Blowing You; Stray Cat Cunt; Stand By Your Gland; Sweet Home 3 Mile Island; Don't Stop (Thinkin' About Interns); All You Need Is Lunch; Lunch Me Do; She Lunches You, Yeah Yeah Yeah!; And I Lunch Her.

HOW YOU CAN USE THIS, FOR REAL
- Headline writer for *People*, *Entertainment Weekly*, etc.
- Writer/Researcher for *Cracked*.

#127 — SOUND EFFECTS

Boink, cha ching, sprackle, creeeek.... finger + mouth + sound = scene stealer. Need we say more?

REMEMBER

Everything you hear is potentially a funny sound.

OTHER COOL SOUND EXAMPLES
- Iron-lung machine
- Rubberized balloon being squeezed by clown
- Cat scratching "shadow balls"

SOUND EFFECTS AND INAPPROPRIATE BEHAVIOR – TOGETHER AT LAST!

Use sounds out of context for x-tra laughs:

- The sound of a blender overlaid on a video of someone masturbating furiously
- The sound of a howler monkey overlaid on a video of someone masturbating furiously
- The sound of a straw being sipped overlaid on a video of someone masturbating – and drinking a shake

#128 — SOUND OF RECORD SCRATCHING TO A HALT

The comedic tool so funny it no longer requires a visual accompaniment! Congratulations! A special thanks to radio commercials and *Malcolm in the Middle* for sticking with this one from its infancy.

HOW YOU CAN USE THIS IN YOUR EVERYDAY LIFE

Let's say you work in an office. It's a family business selling novelty bumper stickers. Your office has an old-fashioned record player and hasn't been decorated since 1979. It needs a lot of work. Office gossip says that in 1979 Old Man Teitelbaum's nephew was one of the Iranian hostages and he felt it was inappropriate to re-decorate the office while Islamic fundamentalist students were holding Americans captive in Iran. Actually, they weren't students at all, but terrorists who believed that the United States of A was a perverted nation whose people were the sons and daughters of the devil. As a matter of fact, they didn't even think women should exist. Which is really ridiculous because without women, where would they be? Do Islamic fundamentalists not have moms? Who cleaned their tushies when they wet themselves when they were little babies? Mohammed? Did Mohammed change their diapers? This whole thing is madness, madness we say. This number might be the least useful to you in your everyday life. Sorry.

#129 — SPORTS HUMOR

Here's the great thing about this number – you don't have to be athletic to use it! Which works out really well for you, because, as with
most of our anticipated demographics, most likely you were the kid
picked last at sports in school and therefore developed some sense
of humor as a defense mechanism against the emotional pain and
humiliation! But we don't want to be exclusive – this information is
insanely valuable ALSO for those of you who WERE picked first for
teams and now find yourselves in the awkward position of trying to
be funny because your athletic prowess and popularity skills have
dwindled. Bottom Line: Creating a funny sports scenario is as easy
as taking a baby – here's the formula:

THE FORMULA FOR ALL SPORTS COMEDIES
1. Idiot/idiots suck at sports.
2. Idiot/idiots thrown into situation in which he/they <u>must</u> play
   sports (e.g., accidentally awarded football scholarship;
   must save sentimental piece of property; wants approval
   from vicious father).
3. Idiot/idiots, against all odds, play in "big game" and,
   against all odds again, win.
4. Vicious father now loves idiot / idiots because they are
   "winners" (use this ending only if you are attempting some
   sort of artistic credibility or pathos, otherwise substitute
   image of fat kid smiling and having chocolate milk poured
   on his head).

STEREOTYPICAL CHARACTERS YOU CAN USE
Gut-hanging-over-belt coach, Seemingly Racist coach, Homophobic
coach, Henry Winkler, Easily Excitable coach, Lovable Loser coach,
Porn Mustache coach, Wise-Yet-Crotchety assistant coach,
Annoying mascot.

HOW YOU CAN USE IT IN BARS
A finely crafted, cutting, expertly worded, smoothly delivered sports
joke can get you punched in the mouth. This is Lakers country!

#130 — SUBTLETY / UNDERSTATEMENT

Here's a FUN exercise! Mix 'n' match #130 with some less obvious numbers. Expands your range!

PRIMO EXAMPLES
- Subtle / wino (#102)
- Understated / voodoo doctor (#164)
- Disciplined / dick joke (#27)
- Reserved / slow-motion fight (#123)
- Nuanced / vomiter (#40)
- Restrained / dummy (#35)
- Suppressed / catchphrase (#14)
- Controlled / devil (#138)
- Restricted / mistaken identity (#79)
- Reined-in / retard (#113)

#131 — SUPERHEROES / CARTOON CHARACTERS

Funniest when asked to do menial tasks, i.e. Green Lantern diapering a baby or Wonder Woman awkwardly purchasing tampons.

OTHER #131 BITS (USUALLY MORE SUCCESSFUL WITH A SEXY ELEMENT)
- Plastic Man / porn star (perfect for #88)
- Galactus / doing his taxes
- Superman / in a world of Supermen and consequently not so super
- The Flash / premature-ejaculation issues
- Spider-Man / dealing with an irritating fly

- Hi and Lois / dementia
- The Justice League of America / crotch rot
- Beetle Bailey / Saigon village raper
- Nancy / as a whore

#132 — SWITCHEROO

A fine "go-to" number – especially when it comes to farce. Adding the "eroo" to the end of what used to be called "the switch" has really given this number more youth and vitality. If you're lucky, at the end of a good switch, um, excuse us, "switcheroo," you should get one world-class #144 (Double Take).

HISTORICAL BIT

John Hancock goes to sign the Declaration of Independence, gets distracted, absently picks up what he thinks is a feather dipped in ink – and signs with nearby Benjamin Franklin's finger! Can bring a boring cabinet meeting back from the ashes!

WHERE YOU'VE SEEN IT BEFORE

The Nixon Administration, and that scene in *Young Frankenstein* where dimwitted bulging-eyed hunchback Marty Feldman takes Abby Normal's brain.

HOW YOU CAN USE THIS IN YOUR REAL LIFE

Let's say you work in an office. If you want to get in good with the rest of the staff at your organic-farm distribution office, try this chicanery on your boss. Whether he/she is an asshole or not, this bit will be high-larious.© One day, bring your boss a small plant as thanks for something he/she did for you – it might seem like you're kissing their ass, but that's okay. Wait two days, and then, without anyone seeing, sneak into the boss's office and substitute the small plant with a slightly larger plant – same planter! Two days later, increase the size of the plant again. Keep doing that every two days until one morning the boss walks into his/her office and there's a full tree on their desk!

Other variations on this switcheroo include slowly changing the race on the people in your boss's family photographs over time and putting a toothpaste-brand label on a tube of Preparation H and slipping it into your boss's not-so-secret-midday-toothbrush-kit... at least your boss's mouth will be free of 'roids!!!

Once you tell everyone that you're responsible for the shenanigans, they'll think you're hilarious. You'll possibly be the most popular salesperson that the organic-farm company has ever seen! Good job!

#133 — THE BEAT

The right timing of a beat makes or breaks a bit... can send even a "knock knock" joke hurtling toward tragedy if not embraced... know the beat, feel the beat, turn the beat around.

THE DIFFERENCE BETWEEN #133 AND #142

To the untrained eye or ear, sure, these seem like the same. But #142 (The Pause) by definition does not need to be followed by something funny on the part of the Pauser. When the Beater throws a Beat into a comedy scene, however, it MUST be followed by a big payoff. Remember this non-palindrome: "Pauses are longer and Beats are specific." (It's fun to remember things, isn't it?)

#134 — THE "BLACKOUT"

An interdisciplinary number that depends primarily on technology and a sense of stage lingo to be effective. A funny way to end a bad date is to simply say "...and Blackout!" and then bow, get in your car, and peel away quickly. In any stage scene, if you're ever in trouble, you can always use the reliable line "I have the cancer" – trademarked by Edward Furman in 1991, but allowed for use in the continental U.S. This will end any scene and hopefully the lighting guy isn't too drunk and is actually listening for the blackout line. Its origins can be traced back to Man's desire to destroy the sun.

IF YOU WANT TO KNOW SOME OF THE LINGO

This number is a good one to memorize and throw out there if you meet up with any improvisers. They will refer to "Blackout" scenes as short sketches/skits (#121, although they won't use the word "skits" – if they DO, then get out of the conversation, fast!) that last for a small amount of time. In stand-up comedy terms, these are "one-liners."

Instead of wasting a lot of energy on the longer pieces, which are difficult because you might have to integrate character development and other stuff, try your novice hands at creating a "blackout."

SAMPLE "BLACKOUT" SCENE FOR YOU TO USE, FREE, BECAUSE YOU PAID MONEY FOR THIS BOOK

Remember to use the K.I.S.S. (Keep It Short & Stupid) method!

[*Two people on stage. One is dressed as a whore, the other as a circus clown with a ZZ Top-like beard, holding an oversized lollipop, a balloon animal with a huge balloon dick, and a poster that says "Free Pee Wee." The clown is nonchallantly stroking the balloon animal's dick. The whore is reading a newspaper.*]

                    WHORE
        It says here that the president said
        "Nucular" again instead of "Nuclear."

                    CLOWN
        I could never be the president.

                    WHORE
        Why not?   This is America — anyone
        could be president.

                    CLOWN
        Nah, I think I'd worry too much about
        embarrassing myself.

[*WHORE and CLOWN both turn their heads quickly to stare at each other and then slowly turn their heads out to the audience and laugh maniacally.*]

                    BLACKOUT

That whole thing, minus laughs, should take about 18 seconds. Now go write your own!!

#135 — THE CALLBACK

The late-night talk show as we know it would surely crumble like so much laugh dust if not for this repetitive time-killer. That's right, laugh dust. The more jokes you can repeat, the fewer jokes you need. Any priest will tell you that's why there's only ten commandments. BE CAREFUL – he may molest you while telling you this. (Beware: priest molestation humor might not be in vogue at the time you are reading this. Check your local scene prior to using this bit.)

EASY-TO-USE-IN-YOUR-OWN-HOUSEHOLD CALLBACK LINES THAT WE CALL "HOUSEHOLD CALLBACKS"

- "Those dishes still aren't done!"
- "The grass isn't getting any shorter!"
- "That homework isn't gonna do those dishes!"

#136 — THE CLERGY

As we write this new "bible of comedy," COMEDY BY THE NUMBERS,© in 2007, making jokes about priests molesting children is like shooting fish in a Catholic barrel. We won't be party to this sad "genre" of comedy, and we strongly suggest that you ONLY write a few priest/pedophile jokes to have in case of an emergency. If you're on stage and appear to be dying, rather than killing, then and only then should you resort to making fun of these pathetic creatures.

CLASSIC CLERGY JOKES

It's still open season on any variation of a joke that starts with "A priest, a rabbi, and a nun walk into a bar…" Go for it! For a writing exercise, we suggest the following combinations with the "…walked into a bar" joke – create your own punch line!

- A priest, a rabbi, and a hooker
- A priest, a rabbi, and a taller rabbi
- A priest, a minister, and a pastor
- A priest, a Hasidic rebbe, and a frog
- A priest, an accountant, and a criminal attorney
- A priest, a toddler, and well, that's it.
  (*Okay, okay, we couldn't help ourselves.*)

CAN I MAKE FUN OF THE CLERGY IN OTHER WAYS THAT DON'T REFERENCE THEIR OVERWHELMING DESIRE TO HARM CHILDREN?

Yes! The other foibles of the clergy, including alcoholism and the constant threat of corporal punishment in religious schools, are still up for comedy grabs. They should be tucked away in your repertoire as deep as Father Tim put his hand up Prof. Hoffman's butt cheeks. (Please note that, for the sake of comedy, Prof. Hoffman bravely put forth his name for use in this line though he is neither religious nor the victim of clerical molestation.)

CLERGY COMEDY AND GOD

Many of the classic jokes involving the clergy ALSO drag God into it. St. Peter and the Pearly Gates are also referenced ad nauseum. This is a great number for you if you're looking to break new ground, but beware − it's tough, and you're taking on a literally sacred cow in society. Not because you should be sensitive or have respect, but mostly because it's so fucking hard to come up with anything new that hasn't already been printed in everything from *Toastmasters* to *Readers* Fucking *Digest*. Good luck and God bless!

#137 — THE DELAYED REACTION

LITTLE-KNOWN FACT: Jack Benny spent all of 1948 responding to everything that happened to him in 1947.

COMEDY FACT!

Ground breaking, diminutive and foul-mouthed 1960s comedienne Totie Fields lost a leg.

#138 — THE DEVIL / HELL

Similar to the Clergy (#136), the Devil is a classic comedy character – he works in many forms for jokes, bits, shtick, etc. Satan, as he is sometimes called, can be seen as grotesque or as a sly, slick sales-man type who walks among us to gather souls. As you write your comedy, try to imagine different forms for Beelzebub (as he is also sometimes called), and different personalities too! Maybe you've got a Devil with a lisp or an insufferable overuse of the word "like" – have fun with The Dark One (yet another nom de plume)!

AS FOR HELL, WE SHARE THE FOLLOWING EXAMPLES FOR COMEDIC HELLS

- At the grocery store, in line behind someone with 13 items in the 12-item express lane.
- At the DMV, in line behind someone who has to spell his or her multi-syllabic Eastern European-no-vowels name to a civil servant trying to type it in for a new driver's license.
- In line at the movies for a hot new film, when the tickets sell out just as you get to the front!
- Standing in line in Russia for toilet paper – or bread – you're not sure which! (But it's a long line.)
- Standing in any line.

BIT

There's a complicated relationship between the Devil and an angel. This comedic device is often tried in comedy sketches where a char-acter has a crucial decision to make and, unsolicited, the Devil shows up on one shoulder to render an opinion of the character's possible course of action while a heavenly angel (halo and all) shows up on the other shoulder, promoting a more positive, often benevolent, choice. The character will often choose the Devil's choice because it's funnier and gives an opportunity to use a powerhouse tag line: "buzz off, fag-angel."

In *Animal House,* for example, the Devil urges a character to fuck a 14-year old girl – the devil is like that.

#139 — THE ELDERLY AND THEIR FOIBLES

There are some facial reactions that the government won't let comedians have until they're 65. The Public's love for the elderly is equally matched by the ease with which we'll laugh at old people talking about sex and their bowel movements. You canNOT hurt your career by finding some old people for your act! Guaranteed!

GET THE ELDERLY IN ON THE JOKE!

Old people, like animals, have a much higher threshold for what embarrasses them, so you're most likely to find a willing ally in your quest for laughs. Many old folks have distinguished themselves in quirky commercials, as sidesplitting characters in major motion pictures, and as crotchety supporting characters on sitcoms – we really owe a lot to them. Thanks, old people!

HOW EVERY COMEDIAN SECRETLY HOPES THEY'LL END UP

The Sunshine Boys – George Burns & Walter Matthau

THINGS YOU CAN HAVE OLD PEOPLE DO ANYTIME, ANYWHERE, AND IT WILL BE FUNNY

- Swear
- "Hit" on young people (not kids; for that, see #136 – okay, we'll stop)
- Walk super slow
- Put on extra talc
- Shit themselves
- Breakdance
- Pretend to have an erection
- Travel in a crowded vehicle
- Do something athletic
- Bitch and complain

> **COMEDY FACT!**
>
> Jackie Gleason battled weight problems his entire life — and lost.

#140 — THE FOIL

The Foil is an essential element of any comedy production. This is the person whose goals are at direct odds with yours. It's ironic, isn't it? Every comedic character (who brings nothing but love to everyone around him) actually <u>needs</u> someone to hate them for a successful comedy experience.

AUDITION TIP

When interviewing for a Foil position, remember to bone up on exasperation, fuming, heavy sighing, fist shaking, cursing, pulling at your hair, stomping up and down, and any other rage/anger-based reactions. If you're to foil for an African-American, being a whitey is enough.

HOUSEHOLD FOILS

- Nanny
- Principal
- Neighbor
- Dog that shits in your yard (<u>you're</u> the foil)
- Society

#141 — THE NICKNAME

Every school kid knows that Jackie Gleason was frequently called "The Great One," but do you recognize these other, less familiar comedian nicknames?

- George Burns / "Rusty"
- Stan Laurel / "The Slippery Phantom"
- Moms Mabley / "Moms"
- Edgar Bergen / "Cheetah Balls"
- The Ritz Brothers / "The who?"

WHY SHOULD I HAVE A NICKNAME?

You don't strictly need a nickname, but like a good improv-group name, having a moniker that "fits" you can go a LONG way towards establishing a comedy career before you even tell a joke! Opposites are often good – the classic example is a really fat guy named "Tiny." We recommend being more creative. While you're at it, it's always smart to come up with a good porn name – not that you have any chance of being in porn – but just to be able to immediately throw out there at a party if the topic turns to porn names.

Now that you brought it up, here are a few porn names for you to use if you can't figure something else out (some of these might already be taken): Dick Von Hardrammer, Frank Van Cockenstein, Eric Spitznagel, Rod Roddy, Heddy Foreskin, Dr. Murray Mandelbaum, Harry Ox Balls, Beefy St. Snatchmagnet, Lord Pumper, Steele Pussystretcher.

#142 — THE PAUSE

Be very careful when trying to create a pause in a comedic routine; you run the risk of the audience thinking you're a #113, or perhaps that you forgot your place and are trying to remember where you were in your own personal "running order." We've seen SO MANY incidents where a pause that went on too long literally sucked the life out of a room. The pause is best used by those at the master level. REMEMBER: Bob Newhart became a master at this number because he was an incredibly boring accountant – it helped!

PRACTICE, PRACTICE, PRACTICE

Try pausing at home with your loved ones. See if they "get" it.

#143 — THE TAKE

Verbally translates into: "what the...?" Steve Martin, when he was alive, was a master of this transcendent bit. In the late '70s, The Take was (no pun intended) overtaken by The Double Take as the primary comedic reaction. It was sad at the time, but needed to happen. However, it's important for you, as a fledging funny person, to realize that without The Take, the Double Take would just be another spasm. Show some respect.

#144 — THE DOUBLE TAKE

One of the masonry units of physical comedy – the chairman of the board of reactionary humor. This comedy device is to one's repertoire what trinkets and beads were to the Native American Indian way back when – once you see it, you must have it! You will need full use of your eyes and eyebrows, mouth, neck, and sometimes ears in order to get the substantial laugh that accompanies this baby.

1.   2.   3.

BUT ME... HOW DO I DO IT??

Easy. Follow this simple example of a typical situation where THE DOUBLE TAKE reaction is set up. Picture this scene:

1. You come home from work and say, "Honey, I'm home" as you're walking through the door.
2. You hang up your fedora and coat and walk into the living room.
3. You pick up your newspaper and sit in your favorite easy chair, barely noticing your wife and dog across the room.
4. Your wife is sitting on the couch wearing a huge piece of cheese as a hat. Your dog, King, is sitting next to her in a push-up bra and crotchless panties.
5. You ask your wife how her day was in a manner that suggests you don't really care.
6. You flip through your newspaper nonchalantly as she answers: "Unusual."
7. You say, "That's nice, dear," in a monotone that befits your lack of interest.
8. As you flip the paper one more time, you glance over at her and King and clearly notice that what they are wearing is inappropriate. It doesn't register in your brain at that moment, though, so you look back at your paper.
9. BUT at the same moment you stop rustling the newspaper, your brain DOES finally register the inappropriateness of their attire, and you pull the paper down to your lap while

snapping your neck back and raising both your eyebrows, widening your eyes, and leaving your mouth agape (open). Your face is expressing how unbelievable it is that your wife is sitting on a couch with a dairy product on her head and your pet is cross-dressing in intimate apparel!!

WHERE DID THE DOUBLE TAKE ORIGINATE?

Interestingly enough, this facial comedy began with the immigrants who brought to America not only a yearning for freedom and democracy but also a sense of reactionary humor bred in the shtetls of Eastern Europe.

WARNING! WARNING! WARNING!

Not to be confused with the other members of the "Take" Family: The Take, The Triple Take, The Quad Take, and the "weird uncle" – The Spit Take. Beware of overuse! Too many Double Takes by one character can be mistaken for a physical affliction such as Tourette's Syndrome – which is, as we all know, the funniest of the chronic spastic conditions, but tiresome nevertheless.

#145 — THE TRIPLE TAKE

Not often used by "real" comedians, but reasonably priced nonetheless. This gymnastically comedic move should only be attempted with a qualified medical team standing by. We say, break the rules of comedy!

You, the comedy reader, can try to climb up to this "K2 of Komedy" slowly, by mastering The Double Take and then adding The Take. Once you've got this baby honed, step back and just wait for the chicks to laugh! (Another Comedy Dating Tip! Free!)

LITTLE KNOWN IMPRESSIVE FACT: In San Francisco, known as the birthplace of the "What the...?" School of Observational Comedy, THE TRIPLE TAKE is traditionally taught by hippies, who, as we all know, are able to work on skyscrapers without fear of falling.

DO I REALLY NEED TO TRAIN FOR THIS?

YES! If you don't, then, well, we won't take it personally, but don't sue us for loss of consortium! History is littered with those who have not taken our advice on this. Littered!

#146 — THE QUAD TAKE
Very, very rare… the only recorded use of this bit is in every Howie Mandel movie.

#147 — THE UNLIMITED TAKE
May only be performed with the knowledge of <u>all</u> numbers; also works as a reaction to Carrot Top's career.

#148 — THE SPIT TAKE
This is the popular crazy uncle in the family that will do anything for a laugh – and get it! The bigger the better here: surprising information must be delivered while unsuspecting character is drinking, sipping soup, taking medicine orally, at a water fountain, etc.… When done correctly, it is impossible not to get a laugh. Danny Thomas is still considered "the shit" for this routine.

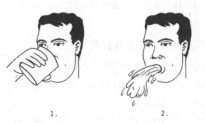

1.   2.

HISTORY LESSON
When The Spit Take came on the scene in the early 1950s, it made the biggest splash in comedy since the catchphrase "I'll bet you my fat ass that's not true!"

WHAT LIQUIDS WORK BEST
- Milk
- Holy Water
- Very very very expensive champagne
- Cum (more of a gel, we know)
- Borscht (because of the pinkish color)
- Kool Aid (especially at mass suicides)
- Split pea soup

AT LAST! HOW TO BE STEVE MARTIN!

The 1st EVER step-by-step breakdown of a career that will last a lifetime! SEE how a Master did it! LEARN why "the banjo" and "white hair" were "good ideas"! HEAR that sound? It's MONEY![1]

"Would've beens" at the ends of their lives are always grousing about how *"if only someone had shown me how,"* they too could've had a glittering career in comedy. Well this page is that "someone."

As anyone in COMEDY will tell you, Steve Martin's is the one career that EVERY comedian WISHES he had! Well, now you CAN have his career — by mimicking it! You too can take an incredible journey, as Steve did, into the comedy history books! And COMEDY BY THE NUMBERS© will be right there beside you!

Please keep in mind that this is a process of DETAILS. Minutiae! ANY deviation from the following easy-to-read steps will lead to failure for your "Steve Martin career." Which is not to say you couldn't have the career of, say, Charlie Callas — fine in its own way, certainly. But we're not here to coddle you. Indeed, we're not your mommas. If you're going to do it, then this is how you will have to do it! Okay? Okay! Now, enter!

PRELUDE: CAREER TIMING

Yes, even your entry to comedy requires diamond-precision accuracy. Mr. Martin has implied on several occasions that his initial triumph as the "Wild and Crazy Guy" was the result of cold-hearted planning. There are no flukes! You see, in the 1970s the country was inundated with overwhelming seriousness (Viet Nam, Watergate, rockstar deaths). There were a lot of things to be mad about, and the comedians of the day reflected that anger in their acts ("Don'tcha hate Viet Nam?"). Steve looked around and figured what the grizzled citizenry needed was an "antidote" of good old American silliness. And he was right. (Also explains disco and the pet rock.) Folks couldn't "get enough" of goofy bits like Happy Feet and Cat Juggling. It seemed like everyone was "getting small." It was the perfect relief from what we were watching on the evening news (napalm, murder, blood, political dissent).

It seems so simple, doesn't it? That's because IT IS.
So what's the mood of the U.S. right now, as you read
this? Is there anger because of robot wars? Is it a Utopia
due to Red and Blue working together as Purple? Is everything in pill form? Whatever society's tone, look for the
opposite (or "Opposite Factor") and run with it.

STEP ONE: BUILDING STEVE MARTIN

Sure, we all know about the catchphrases ("Excuse
me"). But Steve Martin didn't just have jokes — and neither should you. The S.M. "experience" covered all the
angles. ALL of the following individual elements accom-
plished two important things simultaneously:
1. acceptance by the general public
2. a "cool" factor

A) YOUR LOOKS

The White Hair: In your pursuit of "universal
appeal," please save everyone a lot of time and **make sure**
you presently look like a bland everyman — with ONE sly
variation. Something that sets you apart from the herd,
but is also accepted by all. Steve's one variation was
"white hair." Unlike the goatee or pencil moustache,
white hair was something the older set could trust and
the youth thought was just weird enough to be cool. Also,
your haircut should be 100% normal. No corn-rows or
gangsta inscriptions. Once perfection is attained, never
change your look (see below).

The White Suit: We now know that the White Suit was
a ballsy re-invention of the classic "suit comedian" look.
Never before had a color and an article of clothing been so
successfully merged. Except maybe in the medical profession.

> *From the same school:*
> Rodney Dangerfield / red tie
> Pee Wee Herman / red bow-tie, white shoes
> Robin Williams / rainbow suspenders
> Jerry Seinfeld / blue jeans and white "kicks"
> Victor Borge / black tuxedo

B) THE BANJO & THE ROCK AND ROLL CONNECTION

Rock and Roll is how we communicate with our
counter-culture, and is therefore an important ally in
the early stages of a "Steve Martin-like" career.

Hanging out with and dating rock stars is a good foundation, but playing the banjo is what sealed the deal for Steve. Why? Well, first of all, the Youth actually liked the banjo, because it was very similar to the electrical guitar, which their favorite Guitar Gods were then playing. As an added bonus, the Old liked the banjo because of its down-home sound, which reminded them of the "good old banjo days." And was there an underlying connection with *Deliverance*?

We're not sure what the modern equivalent would be, but let us at least discourage you from trying the following instruments:

Drums: because alone, it's just noise
Bass: not in limelight enough
Wind instruments: too homoerotic
Keyboards: too "artsy"
Fiddle: too jaunty
Triangle: triangle = no sex

C) SNL FACTOR

Okay, so you have Steve's looks, material, and, because of a banjo-like instrument, the ability to appeal to the youth market. Now you must "do your thing" on a hip TV comedy show. Steve's appearances on *Saturday Night Live* were nothing less than super-important. Here, in the presence of other comedy gods, he was treated as an equal. A peer. And the adoring counter-culture showered him with money. (Also note: There will exist at this time a great temptation for you to make a movie with one of your lovable *SNL* characters, like *It's Pat!* Steve could have easily made a movie starring the sexual Festrunk Brothers, but he declined, and is respected all the more for it.)

For you today however, it's a very different world. *SNL* (as you should refer to it) is no longer apt to feature an up-and-comer as host. Now, you must already be famous to enjoy this honor. A Buck Henry would not be asked to host in this day and age, because he's old, not a superstar, and is thought to be funny by most people.

STEVE MARTIN CAREER STATUS: Steven Martin was now fast becoming a household name as a stand-up comedian. Throw in several fantastic appearances on Carson and a series of hilarious comedy albums, and you've got a comic who's clearly *made it.* Drink it up! Enjoy yourself! But you SHOULD be thinking about "the future"! <u>And</u> Step Two!

STEP TWO: THE INTRODUCTION OF "DIVERSITY"

Here's where the geniuses branch off from the also-rans, for here is where the seeds of *career longevity* are planted. While Steve was riding high on catchphrases ("Excuse me"), he published a best-selling book (*Cruel Shoes*) and released a successful movie (*The Jerk*). <u>And</u> had a hit novelty record (*King Tut*). He ALSO made a short film that won an Academy Award (*The Absent-minded Waiter*). The public now considered him a writer, movie star, chart-buster, and viable award-winner, AS WELL AS a proven television celebrity — all of which can lengthen a career by years! But stay within the boundaries of what is considered "within your bounds." If you're white, please don't record a rap album. And never <u>ever</u> do anything that includes the words "rock" and "opera."

STEVE MARTIN CAREER STATUS: You're now at the highest peak of your initial success. But here's the question that is currently on the minds of your adoring public: *What do you give the man who's done everything?* <u>Answer</u>: *you ignore him.*

STEP THREE: THE DRY PERIOD

Now that you've hit the highs, there's nowhere to go but down, right? Right. Steve made a series of movie flops (*The Lonely Guy*; *Pennies From Heaven*), *SNL* disbanded, and he was no longer interested in stand-up and comedy records — persuading a fickle public to look elsewhere for yuks. All the white hair in the world won't help you now. This is called a "dry period," and you should have saved enough money to get you through it. (Steve secured the necessary funds by avoiding the typical insane expenditures, e.g. gold made of gold, imported oxygen.)

The Dry Period is when most entertainers freak out and make the kinds of mistakes that will render it <u>impossible</u> for the public to ever accept them back again. The public can sense career nervousness, and once you've lost their respect you'll never regain it. The biggest error? Changing your look. This is not the time to experiment with fads — the movies you make during this period will be embarrassing enough. If your appearance is as Steve Martin's, it is a timeless look, and it will carry you safely through any fly-by-night trends.

Comedians who blew it:

Joe Piscopo / became muscle-bound

The Unknown Comic / started performing without the bag

Any comedian from the 1950s / grew long sideburns to "fit in" in the late 1960s

Bobcat Goldthwait / stopped screaming

STEP FOUR: BACK FROM THE GRAVE

Here's how you get it all back:

1. Team up with another comic legend (Lily Tomlin in *All Of Me*).
2. Write/star in romantic classic (*Roxanne*).
3. Write articles for prestigious publication (*The New Yorker*).
4. Write plays (*Picasso at the Lapin Agile*).
5. Keep doing all of these things until you retire/"die."

Remember that book you wrote in Step Two? Because of that little gem you can now find work as an author. But take the "high road" when selecting a publication to represent, like the *New Yorker*. In comparison, I think we all agree that a regular column in *Punch Fuck* magazine is not the same thing.

STEVE MARTIN CAREER STATUS: Movie-wise, Martin is now in the enviable position of flipping from critic's-darling masterpieces (*Shop Girl*) to "Joe Lunchpail" money-printers (*Cheaper By The Dozen 1 & 2*). Don't you wish you had Steve Martin's career? Well now you HAVE, providing you've followed all steps to the letter!

And take time to help others! If you see someone in the middle of a Step Three and they're about to commit some folly (eyelid piercing, penis splitting), take them aside and gently ask, "What Would Steve Do?"

"Excuse us,"

Prof. Hoffman &. Dr. Rudoren

#149 — THE RULE OF 3s

As it is clearly defined in Webster's dictionary, "three" means "one more than two." (Wow. Those dudes at Webster's aren't putting any extra effort into things, are they? Lazy dictionairiers. Tsk.) Like finger-print evidence being introduced into crime detection, this rule revealed that good comedy was a science.

THE SCIENTIFIC® BREAKDOWN OF THE RULE OF 3s

This theory was recently officially retested at Snickerz Comedy Club in Ft. Wayne, Indiana. The comic was Kip Adotta. Here are the findings:

> **JOKE ADMINISTERED – FIRST TIME:** Yes, it feels like the first time. It feels like the very first time. <u>Big</u> laughs (second only to the final escalation of the joke – the "capper," #3). The audience will love you for intro-ducing them to that rare thing – something truly funny. But be warned: It'll never feel like this again.

> **JOKE ADMINISTERED – SECOND TIME:** The laugh of recognition. As with a second romantic date, a certain amount of heightening is required in this outing (Another Comedy Dating Tip!). Our studies show this is a good place to go with cursing (#24), or repeating a catchphrase (#14) established in the initial delivery – <u>just</u> like on a second date! (Amazingly, Another Comedy Dating Tip!) Sometimes called "The Callback" (#135).

> **JOKE ADMINISTERED – THIRD TIME:** (An audience member thinks:) "*I remember the very first time I laughed at that joke – it was the funni-est thing I'd ever heard. And that second time was just as funny. It felt good to see an old friend. This third time really upped the ante, AND resolved some things. But it was different – the joke must have felt it, too. Yes, we were good for each other for a while there… But I've got other jokes to laugh at. I'm not a one-joke type. Shit, I'm laughing at jokes all over town. Believe it. Move the fuck out of the way. I'm <u>leav-ing</u>, that's why! Jesus! <u>Keep</u> the fucking CD's – I don't fucking care! <u>Psycho</u>!!… I never want to see that asshole joke again.*"

OTHER RULES OF ____

Tragedy comes in fives; pathos comes in one-eighths; rock opera comes in zeroes. (Note the <u>third</u> rule was the "funniest.")

AN EASY WAY TO REMEMBER

3 fingers = 3 rules.

#150 — THE RULE OF 4s

We offer this up as more of a cautionary number than a useful one. We can often learn from the things we SHOULDN'T DO as much as from the things we SHOULD (capitalization is for emphasis).

We know comedy gives so much and asks so little. The least we can do is abide by its rules in an orderly fashion. Comedy comes in 3s. There are absolutely no exceptions to this rule. In fact, <u>nothing</u> should <u>ever</u> be repeated 4 times, including "Help," "I'm dying," and "There's a combine heading right for you."

#151 — THE RULE OF 7s

After the comedy death of the 4s (#150), the inanity of the 5s, and the pure hatred-inducing reaction of the 6s, here's where it finally starts to get funny again. Watch the Pauly Shore vehicle *Encino Man* seven times in a row and you begin to get the picture.

#152 — THE "RUNNER"

Whereas #149 (Rule of 3s) is the theory, this number is the bit itself. If it's funny once, why not three times? That's the principle of this bit: heighten and explore. Very "Level One," but good introduction to padding a show.

CAUTIONARY NOTE: A common misconception is that you need to actually "run." We're not saying that you're stupid if that's what you thought, but maybe you should really read the whole book a few times before you try to be "funny."

HOW YOU CAN USE THIS IN YOUR REAL LIFE

Let's say you work in an office. And your office, like a large percentage of offices, is inside. But it's nice out one day and you want to "work" outside (by "work" we mean lay in the sun, sit on a park bench, and stare at people, or something like that). However, your boss Melanie is anti-you-working-outside. You agree with her because she has the ability to fire you, but you come up with a "bringing the outside in" scheme. The first time we see you post-Melanie's dictum, you are sitting at your desk in your cubicle applying sun block to your face. Melanie walks by and gives you a disdainful look. The second time she walks by, you are holding up a tri-fold reflector on your face with your desk lamp closely hovering over it. Melanie walks by and gives you a disdainful look. The third time in your "I-want-to-go-outside-and-"work"" runner, Melanie happens by just as Ira from sales, a cherub in a Polo shirt, rubs some oil on his hands and begins his back rub of your half-naked body on the floor of your cubicle. Melanie stares, mouth agape, and then rolls her eyes.

#153 — THE SLOW BURN

Works with a #140 (The Foil) very well. This bit, as told to us through British history, was the specific domain of Queen Elizabeth; only after her death was it available to others on a regular basis.

EXTRA FACT! Thanks to COMEDY BY THE NUMBERS,© you need never wonder again who the King of the Slow Burn is. It's Edgar Kennedy in *Duck Soup*! Close second: Corey Haim in *License To Drive*.

HOW DO I MAKE A SLOW BURN?

It's important to realize that this is not JUST about the face! No, you've got to get your whole body involved in a good Slow Burn. Let's say you've just been told that your boss's idiot son totaled your new sports car. You don't want to explode, because, hey, you might lose your job. So you immediately go into SBM (Slow Burn Mode) — you tense up your neck... you squint your eyes... you turn your neck to face the dolt ever so slowly... you grab the rim of your hat if you have one and slowly crunch it against your head... possibly steam comes out through your ears (they can do amazing things with special FX these days)... you hunch your shoulders up... maybe a button pops of your collar… you growl a bit… AND THEN YOU HOLD THE TENSION!

Eventually, you know you'll have to pull out of it because there's nothing you can do to the kid – you'll get your ass canned! But YOU'LL get the laughs, not that little shitwaste.

FREE ADVERTISING FOR EDGAR KENNEDY!

#154 — THE SLOW FADE

As with the #134 (The Blackout), this number will bring you into direct contact with "The Lighting Guy" – a humor club/theatre staple. This dude is practically your alcoholic comedy partner. For he is the one "editing" your show/routine – which, using comedy math, works out to about 50% of your act! That's how important he is!

THE HORRIBLE IRONY

The beers you must buy The Lighting Guy – in order to get him on your good side, thereby assuring his "want" to not fuck up your cues – may actually turn out to be the very thing that distracts him from doing just that!

TIP!
What are you, some sort of funny guy?

The history of comedy is closely associated with the history of labels. (Labels were first introduced by the ancient Canadians who found them helpful in the new society they created when they broke away from the United States.)

Over the years, historians have realized that besides just a hook°, a comedian can have that "label" that makes him/her stand out in a crowd.

When one goes far back and examines the history of comedy, one begins to see certain patterns, motifs and themes that seem to crop up over and over again. (Amazingly, this is true in other professions as well. For instance, did you know nearly all US Presidents have worn tie clips?) Join us as we employ the popular "list" format. Everyone will be impressed by the names you choose to memorize below.

Under which classification do you belong?

CIGAR COMEDIANS - Groucho Marx, George Burns, Ernie Kovacs, Bill Cosby, Alan King, Sid Caesar, Lou Costello, David Letterman, Milton Berle, Red Skelton, W.C. Fields, Jim Belushi.

MOUSTACHE COMEDIANS - Chester Conklin, Freddie Prinze, Bernie Mac, Billy Bevan, Dan Aykroyd (early career only!), Charlie Chaplin, Steve Harvey, Harold Lloyd (as Lonesome Luke only!), Charley Chase, Raymond Griffith, Peter Sellers (as Inspector Clouseau only!), Ernie Kovacs, Jeff Foxworthy, Sarah Silverman, Cedric the Entertainer, John Cleese (*Fawlty Towers* only!), Oliver Hardy, W.C. Fields (early career only!), Snub Pollard, Richard Pryor, Groucho Marx (fake and real!), Ben Turpin, Eddie Murphy, Paul McCartney (Sgt. Pepper only!).

GLASSES COMEDIANS - Harold Lloyd, Al Franken, Neil Simon, Jack Benny, Ford Sterling, Charley Chase, Woody Allen, Drew Carey, Tom Davis, David Cross, Groucho Marx, most of the Firesign Theatre.

CRAZY HAIR COMEDIANS - The Three Stooges, Yahoo Serious, Carrot Top, Harpo Marx, Gallagher, Gallagher 2, Alfalfa, Larry David, Steven Wright, Marty Allen

FUNNY THOUGH NOT JEWISH - Oliver Hardy, Monty Python, Lucille Ball, John Belushi, Lou Costello, Bob Odenkirk, Cheech and Chong, Bob Hope, Red Skelton, Richard Pryor, Janeane Garofalo, Ernie Kovacs, Jackie Gleason, Buster Keaton, Harold Lloyd, Steve Martin, Martin Short, Smothers Brothers, Andy Kaufman (half), David Letterman, Moms Mabley.

FUNNY THOUGH JEWISH - Myron Cohen, Jack Benny, [*18 pages deleted here - Ed.*], Al Jolson.

THE COLOR OF COMEDY - Red Buttons, Red Skelton, Red Sandwich, Slappy White, Blue Man Group, Carrot Top, Tom Green, Ben Blue, Pink Lady.

COMEDY'S REAL NAME - Danny Kaye/David Daniel Kaminsky; Chico Marx/Leonard Marx; Harpo Marx/Adolph Marx; Groucho Marx/Julius Henry Marx; Gummo Marx/Milton Marx; Zeppo Marx/Herbert Marx; Woody Allen/Allen Stewart Konigsberg; Red Buttons/Aaron Chwatt; Rodney Dangerfield/Jacob Cohen.

THE ROUTINES THAT MADE THEM - Sid Caesar: war-movie routine; Danny Kaye: Tchaikovsky routine; Red Skelton: Guzzler's Gin routine; W.C. Fields: pool-table routine; The Three Stooges: poke-in-the-eye routine; Abbott and Costello: Who's on First? routine; George Carlin: seven-dirty-words routine; Gallagher: Sledgamatic routine; Steve Martin: Excuuuse Me! routine; Bill Saluga: Ya' doesn't has ta call me Ray routine.

TEAMS / TROUPES - Smith and Dale, Abbott and Costello, The Goons, Martin and Lewis, Monty Python, The Kids in the Hall, Olsen and Johnson, The Three Stooges, The Marx Brothers, Kathy and Mo, Laurel and Hardy, Lemmon and Matthau, Aykroyd and Belushi, Farley and Spade, Wayland Flowers and Madam, Burns and Allen, Rowan and Martin, Burns and Schreiber, Shields and Yarnell, Reiner and Brooks, Bob and David, The Hudson Brothers, The Bowery Boys/Dead End Kids, Holmes and Yoyo, The Not Ready For Primetime Players, Tenspeed and Brownshoe, The Ritz Brothers, Bergen and McCarthy, Willie and Lester, Method Man and Redman, SCTV, The Mommies, The Firesign Theatre, Cheech and Chong, Ozzie and Harriet, The Upright Citizens Brigade, The Rat Pack, Wilder and Pryor, Owens and Clark, Hope and Crosby, Hoffman and Rudoren, Hudson and Day, Cook and Moore, Mad TV, The Goodies, Gleason and Carney, Sonny and Cher, Donny and Marie.

COMEDY BY THE… LETTERS! - SCTV, UCB, MADTV, SNL, U2

#155 — TRANSPORTATION VEHICLES

Write these down: Putting a car in R and then driving F; put-upon driving-school instructor; car falling apart piece-by-piece over a long chase scene; too many people in the car; cab drivers who are foreign (see #95 for hi-jinx).

SOME FUNNY VEHICLES

Herbie; My Mother the Car; Columbo's "ride"; the Munsters' cars (more cool than funny); the Beverly Hillbillies' jalopy (especially when it was converted into a James Bond-like "spy car"); Starsky & Hutch's El Camino; the coconut car that the professor invented; anything by famed car-designer George Barris (see signed photo below).

The King – George Barris. I believe the Inscription reads, "To Eric – Aw shucks Man —G. Barris 3"

"NOT FUNNY" VEHICLES

The car Kennedy was assassinated in; Bonnie & Clyde's car; James Dean's car; any boxcar to Auschwitz; Jayne Mansfield's car; this is turning into a real downer...

COMEDY FACT!

W.C. Fields hated children and animals and, due to alcoholism, acquired dreaded "gin blossoms" on his nose.

#156 — TRAVELING BITS / SCENARIOS

Could be used with a #157, but is much more involved. There's no shortage of yuks when you squeeze two fat guys into a train compartment. Actually, fat people traveling on <u>anything</u> too small is funny – especially because the government says fat people should not be allowed to travel.

WHERE YOU'VE SEEN THIS BEFORE

The groundbreaking film *Silver Streak* featured Gene Wilder and Richard Pryor as both black and white people (funniest train film since Fred Silverman's Grand TV Experiment *Super Train,* which was like the *Love Boat* except on a train instead of a boat of love).

ANY OTHERS?

Another outstanding comedy film is *Planes, Trains, and Automobiles* featuring Steve Martin, the late John Candy, and the infamous line "Those aren't pillows!" (see #57 reference).

comedy classics collector's stamps

CLIP 'EM AND COLLECT 'EM!

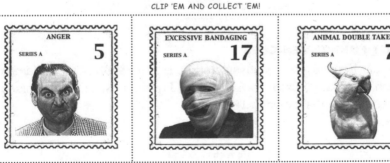

Do not attempt to lick.

#157 — TWO OR MORE PEOPLE TRYING TO GET THROUGH A DOOR AT THE SAME TIME

A classic "Writes Itself" scene! Ideally, one of the two people is morbidly obese. If you're not lucky enough to find obese people (quite frankly, it's insanely easy), then it'll still work, but will feel lacking.

HOW YOU CAN USE THIS IN YOUR REAL LIFE

Let's say you work in an office. You not only "work" there, but you're one of the bosses. You often have people come into your office to meet with you about the great decisions you're making to keep the company profitable. Good job! This number could be worthwhile for your OWN amusement, or, if you can time it appropriately, for the amusement of a select few. The key is timing. At a certain point in the day, figure out which two employees are exactly the same distance from the door to your office. Take into account the smoothness of their travel and body-mass index. Then call them both up and ask them to come to your office. At the end, tell them to make it right away and that you'll be "timing them." God willing, both of these knuckleheads will end up trying to squeeze through your 32"-wide doorway at the same time. The key is to buzz your secretary right after you summon these employees and tell her/him to "watch what's gonna happen at my office door in a minute!"

A GREAT BIT TO USE TO BECOME FUNNY, POPULAR, AND SEEMINGLY FIT

When trying to impress a girl at a party, just wait near any door while the others drink. As a fat person approaches, pretend to try to go through the door with them (A GREAT Comedy Dating Tip!).

SADLY

Although he tried to specify 48"-wide doors in all his contract riders, this is the bit that finally drove Louie Anderson out of comedy.

#158 — UGLY PEOPLE

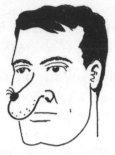

SUBCATEGORY A: MAKING FUN OF YOUR OWN UGLINESS

As Society graciously reminds us, everyone is ugly. And in need of expensive pretty-ing. Would a Phyllis Diller make it in today's "I demand beauty" world? <u>Of course she would!</u> America needs her one Lovable Ugly Chick as much as she needs her one Sexy Fat Guy or her one Bald Leading Man. The career advice is staring you in the face, ugly! You should become the <u>new</u> Phyllis Diller! But remember, the public requires only ONE Diller at a time. So if you've ever imagined yourself involved in one of those great famous show-biz intrigues – where an up-and-comer blackmails and manipulates their competition out of the biz on their way to the top – then <u>now</u> would be the proper time to put this fantasy into action! Not that we recommend it. However, your autobiography (see below) can't <u>just</u> be about your "breathing glue from a sack" addiction.

TANGENTIAL SUGGESTION OF GOOD AUTOBIOGRAPHY TITLES

- (Your name): *The Winner*
- *Why? Why? Why? Why?*
- *Who I Fucked*
- *100 Crossword Puzzles... <u>AND</u> My Life Story!*
- *I Apologize For Winning*
- *Memories of Dreams of Winning*
- *My Year of the Turd*
- *We Regret To Inform You...*
- *Saved!*
- *I'm Nice.*

SUBCATEGORY B: MAKING FUN OF AN UGLY PERSON

Unless you're currently America's number-one Charming Asshole (see below), making fun of an ugly person can make you "the bad guy" in an audience's eyes – **which can lead to financial ruin**. Make sure the ugly person is "set up" as having abusive morals and a lousy nature. This gives you "permission" to insult and hate them, a la #68 (Making Fun of Someone's Flaws).

TANGENTIAL "CHARMING ASSHOLE" HALL OF FAME

- Archie Bunker
- Sean Connery as gentleman spy James Bond
- Charles Grodin
- Chevy Chase (and anyone who copies him, i.e. Ryan Reynolds, Charles Rocket)
- Bill Murray (and anyone who copies him, i.e. early Tom Hanks, early Bruce Willis, early Michael Keaton)
- The cast of *Animal House* (and any film that copies it, i.e. *Caddyshack, Spring Break, Up The Academy*)
- Tommy Lee Jones (from *The Fugitive* on)
- David Letterman
- Jack Nicholson
- Any small-town sheriff
- Roddy McDowell

NOTE: Being truly ugly (i.e., hard to look at, wince-inducing, comparable to hideous animals) may not be an "automatic" (automatic laugh-getter), but it practically guarantees the arrival of the #95 (Pathos a.k.a. Chaplin Syndrome), which turns "ugly" into "smugly" – as in "smugly awaiting an Oscar!"

COMEDY FACT!

Milton Berle stole jokes, bedded Marilyn Monroe, and was rumored to have the biggest penis in show biz aside from F-Troop's Forrest Tucker. He later died.

#159 — UNDERWEAR

Your go-to laugh when all else fails. Nothing brings you down to the common man's level quicker, and more reliably, than stripping to your skivvies. And your instincts are correct: a "sexy" dance is a great follow-up!

Funny.

A PERSONAL ANECDOTE REVEALED!

A comedy peer of the authors once appeared in a sketch in Chicago clad only in his underwear. The roars were immediate and lengthy. It wasn't until backstage that the friend realized his dingus-stick had been hanging out for all to see throughout. The friend's sober summary: "I knew nobody's that funny."

HOW YOU CAN USE THIS IN YOUR EVERYDAY LIFE

Let's say you work in an office. You've heard of "casual Fridays"? Well, picture that it's been a long week and you're pretty darn proud of yourself because you finally got Old Man Henderson to sign off on your big new filing-system idea. What better way to celebrate and/or gloat over your office rivals then by showing up on that "casual" Friday with some comedy underwear! Chicks (or guys) will think you're hilarious and will laugh at you – in the good way that you WANT to be laughed at! Have some snappy comebacks at the ready, like "Boxer? I didn't even KNOW her" or "Let me be brief…" or "Boy, he ran away from this water cooler so fast, he left SKIDMARKS!"

**FUNNY THINGS THAT CAN BE WRITTEN ON UNDERWEAR
SHOW THAT YOU ARE NOT AFRAID TO REFERENCE YC**
GENITAL SIZE OR SEXUALITY IN PUBLIC

- Home of the Whopper (men)
- I Voted for Bush (lesbians and/or men)
- Jurassic Dick (kids will love this one)
- Mmmm... Sack Lunch (blue collar)
- Vote Re-pubic-an! (Republicans)
- Shaved and Ready for Work! (White collar women)
- My Other Crotch is a Pussy (transsexuals)

#160 — UNINTENTIONALLY FUNNY

We know that you're going to try awfully hard to make something either FUNNY or NOT FUNNY. But it's hard to control sometimes. We suggest you experiment with these borderline bits: real life; reading this book at an execution; Stallone movies; hip TV shows; politicians with bad rugs; the corrections page of the *NY Times*; Spain; proposing marriage in a body cast; clown with cancer; Michael Jackson's dick; Jerry Lewis's career.

HOW WILL I KNOW THE DIFFERENCE?

If you were hoping that someone would cry at the end of your scene where the circus clown dies of tongue cancer and, instead, the audience cracks up as Busto (or whatever name you give him) dies pointing to a glass of water, then you've failed – or have you?

SOMETIMES you want to shoot for unintentionally funny just to cover your bases!

COMEDY FACT!

Animal House director John Landis was completely cleared of any involvement in the tragic helicopter-blade beheading of actor Vic Morrow and two small children on the set of his film *Twilight Zone - The Movie.* He later directed *The New Munsters.*

TIP!

*There are two things comedians LOVE: one, the sound
of a room full of people laughing at their act;
and two, the sound of their own voice.*

Funny people tend to run in the same circles. They'll hit the same bars after a show. They'll eat at the same IHOP together. They are often caustic and feral (good comedy words).

We don't want to sound pushy, but if you want to be one of THOSE types of funny people, then you'll have to learn what to say to other funny people who have grasped the math of comedy.

We can't speak for EVERY social situation, but in most cases, comedians in the wild like to engage in the culture of what comedians call "cut downs." If you want to be viewed by others as truly funny, there is no better way than to learn to "cut down" other people and pick on their flaws and fears.

Hate-filled retorts are often the language — and the currency — of the comedian in his/her element.

For most true comedians, including you I'm sure, these hurtful phrases and references will be easy to learn — remember, inside every funny person is a hurt child looking to strike back at "daddy" for the perceived injustices he/she has suffered!

Here are just a few of the government-approved barbs that you can toss back to some feeble comedian to "put them in their place" - AND gain their respect!

1. "Your elbow was really funny tonight, really."

2. "I wish my dog was as funny as you, I'd shoot him in the face."

3. "Finally! A comedian who's not afraid to suck."

4. "Your type of comedy will never go out of style, because it's never been IN STYLE!"

5. "You were goddamn horrible."

#161 — VENTRILOQUISM

As far as comedy partners go, you could do a lot worse than a dummy. Think of it! You decide what your partner does, says, and sounds like, everything!! Now that's power! Real power! He will <u>never</u> say anything <u>you</u> don't want him to! What could be more perfect!! Unless, of course... he begins to speak... without you...

WHERE YOU'VE SEEN IT BEFORE

Edgar Bergen & Charlie McCarthy; Willie Tyler & Lester; Jeff Dunham and Peanut; the movie *Magic; Mr. Show*'s East Coast/West Coast Ventriloquist Wars; that classic episode of *Twilight Zone* with what's-his-name and that thing.

#162 — VERBAL ABUSE / SHOUTING

If your brooding, quiet characters aren't receiving the guffaws that they should, try a shouting, angry, and abusive character! Almost everything is funnier when shouted, i.e. cancer-test results, food orders, directions to church, pick-up lines, etc. And NEVER waste an opportunity to insult another character/person – the audience laughs while thinking "Thank G-d that's not me!!"

Originated by the Spanish during the Inquisition as the first method of interrogation, it was discovered to crack up the prisoners. Thus, ipso facto, it led to the invention of numerous means of PHYS-ICAL torture! (See #25.)

Also HIGH-larious© when used by #14s and #87s.

WHERE YOU'VE SEEN IT BEFORE

Great example is in *Monty Python and the Holy Grail* – memorize this passage below and you'll be a hoot at any party with 40-year old comedy nerds:

> "You English Kaniggets! I faht in your general direction!" (Then hit yourself on the head back and forth with each hand.) Guaranteed laff.©

WHERE THIS WILL WORK FOR YOU

Any social situation where you are trying to be popular. There is nothing funnier to the "in crowd" than someone who is loud and abusive.

CAN I MAKE A CAREER IN COMEDY WITH THIS ALONE?

No.

COMEDIANS WHO EMBRACE THIS BIT

- Sam Kinison (dead)
- Jackie Gleason (dead)
- Don Rickles (Vegas)

TWO ORIGINAL EXAMPLES FOR YOU TO MEMORIZE AND CLAIM AS YOUR OWN

- "So, you're the nutless jamoke that's been diddling my wife! I thought this place smelled of jerk!" (*Super Funny if said in a confessional*)
- (*In a doctor's office waiting room, yelling*) "I said... you're pregnant, Sister Mary Katherine!!"

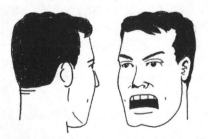

#163 — VOICE OVER SOMETHING THAT CAN'T TALK

Suspension of disbelief fuels this comedy nugget. "I may be an ottoman, but I've got feelings too!" Ha, ha, ha (FREE IDEA: for example the ottoman might have a Turkish accent). Another example: Try imagining what kind of voice your pubic-hair-covered soap dish would have!

OR TRY THESE OBJECTS / VOICES
- Double-D bra / gay Southern writer
- Important paperwork your boss needs tomorrow / stoner
- Your penis / French lover
- Your vagina / black lover
- Salad bar / voice of unhealthy fried-chicken pan in disguise

#164 — VOODOO

Voodoo is an ancient religion practiced primarily by blacks in places like Haiti and parts of New Orleans. Easily the wackiest of religions, throw a white person into a voodoo scene and they'll run like crazy in fear — while YOU LAUGH!

MOST FAMOUS VOODOO BIT

Make a doll of another character (your nemesis) that you would like to annoy. Put doll in funny mini-version of an outfit worn by your rival. Take needles and poke doll. Reaction will be High-larious.© ALSO: remember that people from Haiti speak funny on purpose to make themselves feel better.

WHERE YOU'VE SEEN IT BEFORE

Remember that Abbott & Costello scene where they each had dolls of the other and started poking needles in the doll to get back at each other and then they reacted physically in the place on their body where the needle was going into the doll? It was funny to watch that.

The original Goons: Secombe, Bentine, Sellers, Milligan

The Goon Show answers the question: "Where did Peter Sellers come from?" Few in America today are aware of just how important this show was/is. It is currently **the greatest radio comedy show ever made.** From 1951 to 1960 this <u>insanely</u> funny program was broadcast over BBC Radio. "Goonery" quickly became a British national treasure (and still is). Everybody loved "the Goons," from the Queen down.

The players: Spike Milligan, Peter Sellers, Harry Secombe (and Michael Bentine in the early days). They were called "Surrealists of Sound." The Goons all met in the Army during World War II, where they cultivated a healthy mistrust of authority types, and had a shared life view and awareness of "the absurdity of it all."

> <u>Spike Milligan:</u> Wrote the scripts. Although they all shared the same sense of crazy humor. With Sellers, provided most of the voices.

> <u>Peter Sellers:</u> This is where his quick-change, chameleon-like ability to inhabit different "beings" blossomed. He regularly played a minimum of five characters an EP. It is truly amazing to hear.

> <u>Harry Secombe:</u> Provided the perfect "boob as hero" — but his character Neddie Seagoon was no straightman. Absolutely everyone was funny on this program.

The show: Here's why it's great. Each half-hour episode (recorded in front of a live audience) effortlessly blended the following:

- Hilarious wordplay influenced by the Marx Brothers (with enough brilliant zingers to fill a "stateroom scene")
- Absurd situations and characters partly-influenced by Alice in Wonderland
- And a Warner Bros. Cartoon sensibility with regards to pacing, violence and sound effects (e.g., the sound of a piano driving over the ocean).

Much like Python later, the show often had to fight for *quality control* with the higher-ups at the Beeb.

Who they influenced: Practically every British comedian and, whether they're aware of it or not, practically every other comedian on the planet. The Goons influenced *A Show Called Fred* and *Q5*, which influenced Python, which influenced *Saturday Night Live*, which influenced this book, which is now influencing YOU.

The characters: Low on catchphrases per se (the Goons hated them), but the voices themselves became catchphrases with the public — all were Mel Blanc-good. Each was a variation of the insane man-child; from cowardly military officers to idiots so stupid they could barely speak. Seagoon, Bluebottle, Flowerdew, Hercules Grytpype-Thynne, Henry Crun, Eccles, Nugent Dirt, Moriarty, Dr. Londongle, and Major Bloodnok (and a clipped, vomiting-sounding voice simply called "Throat").

Highlight episodes: Such epic adventures as The Phantom Head-Shaver, Foiled By President Fred, The Dreaded Batter Pudding Hurler, The Affair of the Lone Banana, Napoleon's Piano, and The House of Teeth.

"So you're saying it's still worth listening to today": Yes — we're not some old fool globbering on about fruit prices here! Trust us, goonery fits in more with today's humor than when originally broadcast. The jokes hold up (apart from the occasional topical reference) and the whole thing has a psychedelic quality. *The Goon Show* is the real thing. CDs are available through the BBC website, but there's only one true visual representation of what they did — the video of "The Last Goon Show of All."

So, thank you, *Goon Show*.
Comedy couldn't have done it without you.

#165 — WEDDINGS

Only rule for a humorous wedding scene: You need one of these three things — puking groomsmen, stuttering priest, or incontinent bride.

HOW YOU CAN USE THIS IN YOUR REAL LIFE

Let's say you're in a wedding. If you really want to have fun, you have to be prepared to have the bride never ever forgive you for the prank you pull. That said, there's an upside to that too! Your buddy Bruce is getting married to a girl who no one likes. No one. But somehow she has Bruce wrapped around her finger. In order to become memorable, popular, AND break up a doomed marriage, you prepare a plan. You'll steal the identity of your friend's fiancée, pay a hooker (make sure it's not one you've used on any other pranks) to impersonate her around town and cancel all the food, the band, the catering hall, etc. Hookers sometimes don't have good memories, so you might need to practice with her before you send her out. Two days before the wedding, play dumb and ask the future bride if she knows what time the catering hall will be available for you and the other guys to set up the chuppa, or bridal canopy, for the ceremony. When she goes to check with the people, she finds out that "she" cancelled the wedding! You then get to be the confident groomsman who helps solve all her problems — bonus! Eventually, they get married in the office you work in — you've got the keys and access to all the paper products that they use for parties. As the sub-standard party is in "full swing," you spring it on your newly married friends that you personally saved them thousands of dollars by getting a hooker to steal her identity and cancel everything — you're a hero! Or so you think. There probably will be some people who laugh once all this information gets out there.

> **COMEDY FACT!**
>
> Steve Allen hosted the Tonight Show, wrote many books, composed many songs, married Jayne Meadows, made numerous speaking engagements, and died.

#166 — WHITE TRASH

If you're making a white-trash joke, you might be white trash!

BUT WHY JEFF FOXWORTHY?

This is a question that people ARE STILL trying to figure out!

You can't knock him, though. You have to admire his tenacity in finding JUST THE RIGHT gullible subculture and exploiting it. You go, Jeff. Seriously, you go.

WHY DO SOUTHERNERS ALWAYS SOUND KIND OF STUPID?

This is an age-old question! Of course, there have been smart southerners – Jeff Davis and others – but if you want to pick a subculture to mock, you can do worse than selecting the poor, ignorant southern bastard!

SELECT ITEMS TO INCLUDE IN ANY POTENTIALLY FUNNY WHITE-TRASH HUMOR

- Doublewide Trailer
- Your sister
- Your uncle with a gun
- Your aunt with a huge bosom
- Your pappy with a gun
- Your momma who's your aunt
- A dog (preferably old)
- Distinctive smell
- Ignorant hatred of African Americans
- Ability to make "mark" on page

#167 — "WHO'S ON FIRST?"

The first question of comedy! This phrase has become a virtual verbal "secret handshake" for comedy nerds. AND many a cocksman has started on his road to "success" by the memorization of this seminal Abbott & Costello routine. Some have attempted unsuccessful parodies – "Hu's on First?" (Chinese), "Stew is on First?" (stand-up comedians), and "Jews on First?" (Jews playing baseball? right). Try to get a buddy to do this bit with you; the good thing is that you really don't need to be super-fat like Costello.

#168 — WIGS

MOST URGENT! AN IMPORTANT REMINDER! Never lend your comedy wigs to a fellow performer. Remember, "A wig gets <u>one</u> laugh a show" — make sure it's yours. Unless it's a chick. (Another Comedy Dating Tip!)

Funny.   *Funnier.*   *Funniest.*

#169 — WOMEN

Now this one we might get in trouble for (for speaking the truth!), but hear us out. Our society has a long history of women, some of whom have been funny. Phyllis, Gracie, Lucy, Carol, Janeane, Imogene, Vickie, Sarah, Elaine, Lily, Tracey, Moms, Mary, Gilda, Totie, Bonnie, Joan, Wanda, Whoopi, Lucille, Amy, Rachel, Tina, Jodi, Susie, Megan, the other Sarah, Laura, Paget, Maya, Kristen — to name just half of the funny women ever. If you get a chance to use a broad (they also like "dame") in your comedy bit, you should try to do so — if only to get a shot at nailing them. (Incredibly, Another Comedy Dating Tip!) If you happen to BE an actual woman and you're reading this, well, congratulations on getting away from the house and the kids! We're excited for you and hope you can find the time to either learn a little something about comedy or learn enough to support the man of the house!

TO MEN (OR WOMYN)

If you just want to be popular with women and aren't just interested in them as comedy devices, then learn some good jokes to use on them to get them to like you — publicly, they all say they love a sense of humor (privately, studies have shown that they tend to lie and exaggerate, so it's best to have a non-comedy body too).

HOW TO BEST USE A WOMAN

There are so many numbers that work EVEN BETTER when a woman is used! Here are a few for handy reference:

With a #8 BLIND DATE – almost a requirement for heterosexual-based humor.

With a #24 CURSING – somehow, someway, guys love to hear women curse! Try combining #169 and #24 with a #139 (The Elderly & Their Foibles) and now you've got a golden-nugget comedy bit of an old woman cursing like a horny sailor at P-town.

With a #46 FART NOISE – as we all believe, women (except for Sarah S.) don't fart, so the unbelievable, sci-fi-like experience of having a woman fart is laff-ranteed to provoke laughs.

WHERE YOU'VE SEEN IT (THEM) BEFORE

Rarely do movies top the hilarity of *Beaches*. On TV, check out *The Lucy Show, Here's Lucy, Lucy, I Love Lucy, The Mary Tyler Moore Show, Mary, Mary Hartman, Mary Hartman, Wonder Woman, The Carol Burnett Show, Rhoda, Phyllis, Roseanne, Maude, Angie, Alice, Cybil, Sybil, Flo, Hazel, Grace Under Fire, The Nanny, Nanny & The Professor, The Ghost & Mrs. Muir, Cagney & Lacey, Pink Lady & Jeff, One Night in Paris, Bewitched, Hart to Hart, Steel Magnolias, Ab Fab.*

comedy classics collector's stamps
CLIP 'EM AND COLLECT 'EM!

Warning: Stamp perforation not real.

WHEW!

WELL, THAT'S A LOT OF INFORMATION WE JUST GAVE YOU!

THE SEQUEL (GOD WILLING) WILL START WITH #170.

AREN'T YOU SITTING THERE F'ING AMAZED AT HOW MUCH YOU JUST LEARNED?

COMEDY TEST

Now that you've learned EVERYTHING THERE IS TO KNOW
ABOUT COMEDY (barring a sequel), it's time to test
how much you've retained.

SCORE

    100% — See you at the Friar's Club.

    99 to 76% — Role in Christopher Guest movie.

    75 to 51% — Sitcom with your name in title.

    50 to 26% — SNL.

    25 to 0% — Please, won't you read the book again?

BEGIN... HERE

1. Subtlety does not work with:

    A) dick jokes

    B) shit jokes

    C) nag jokes

    D) jokes

2. The first rule of improvisation is:

    A) "Yes, and..."

    B) "No."

    C) do old material

    D) laugh at your own performance

3. "Bill Titwhisker" is a funny name. True or false?

4. In a "can't get to sleep" routine, which bit wouldn't work?

    A) swallowing a bottle of No-Doze

    B) shouting at noisy neighbors

    C) a deal with the devil

    D) irony

    E) conducting a monkey orchestra

5. Complete the following statement for maximum comedic effect: "I don't care if you are my landlord, you ____!

    A) asshole
    B) fag-dicker
    C) piss-marryer
    D) cunt-fuck fuck-head

6. Which one of the following is not unintentionally funny?

    A) retards
    B) hobos
    C) gays
    D) cast of Mad TV

7. "Forced to dress in drag" is the funniest comedic premise ever invented. True or false?

8. Menstruation jokes are only funny to:

    A) women
    B) women and women
    C) both
    D) sparrows
    E) all womankind

9. The perfect "capper" to a chase sequence is:

    A) animal double take
    B) drunk looks at his bottle and throws it away (gives up booze for life)
    C) the gangsters chasing you explode
    D) hide in costume shop, reemerge in "Swiss Miss" getup
    E) all of the above
    F) none of the above
    G) some of the above
    H) one or two of the above
    I) none of the above, but something below

10. The inclusion of drug humor in your act will ensure that you will be:

   A) popular with a younger demographic
   B) "edgy"
   C) under investigation for the rest of your life
   D) considered a druggie, so you might as well be one for real
   E) eventually on Oprah

11. In a comedy script, which of the following sound-effect words would you use to describe a fart noise? List them in order of preference:

   A) POOT!
   B) FLOOP!
   C) BZZZZZZZ!
   D) NIXON!
   E) SSSHIT!
   F) BLAP!
   G) MAGAZINE!
   H) FFFFFFF!
   I) PWEET!
   J) HUMPHRIES!
   K) THORNT!
   L) POP!

12. SOLVE THE PROBLEM:
   You have an audition for SNL in which you must present 3 funny characters. You've already decided on 2 characters: the current president and a TV-commercial huckster. Which is the best choice for your third character?

   A) a man-child who has difficulty picking up girls (has catchphrase)
   B) doofus lounge singer (has catchphrase)
   C) the funniest character ever created (has no catchphrase)
   D) impression of celebrity who has catchphrase
   E) a very unfunny character with 8 catchphrases

13. The "sound of a record scratching to a halt" wasn't funny the first time it was used, and it still isn't funny. True or false?

14. Using the rules of anti-comedy, which is the best way to "deconstruct" the following bit?

You're brandishing a bucket which the audience believes is filled with water. You then throw its contents at the audience — but instead of water the bucket is really filled with:

A) confetti
B) shit
C) bourbon
D) miniature buckets
E) bottles of water
F) cassettes of Abbott & Costello's "Who's On First?"
G) videos of a Harlem Globetrotters game

15. Racial jokes are not funny when presented by:

A) white joke books
B) whitey
C) crackers
D) Hitler's joke book

16. To be a "cross-eyed comedian" you must give up which of the following:

A) ever being taken serious
B) real respect from a woman
C) authority of any kind
D) all of the above and more

17. "Clumsy shtick" is required in all comedy movies. True or false?

18. SOLVE THE PROBLEM:

    You're a tall, handsome straightman/woman searching for a partner to form a comedy duo with. Which one is the best choice for your "funny man/woman"?

    A) a short, fat stooge
    B) a comedian named "Blackhater"
    C) a slut
    D) any asshole off the street

19. Comedy + Pathos = acting awards. True or false?

20. A comedian should have how many comedy wigs on hand?

    A) 1
    B) 3
    C) 10
    D) 12,000

21. A president who mispronounces words and can't form sentences is an example of what kind of comedy?

    A) political humor
    B) "someone where they shouldn't be" routine
    C) anti-comedy
    D) "the elderly and their foibles" humor
    E) scare comedy

15 MINUTE BREAK

22. Benny Hill is funny because:

    A) he laughs at his own jokes
    B) he's naughty
    C) he smacked the old bald guy on the head
    D) he's British
    E) he smiles a lot

23. SOLVE THE PROBLEM:

    You are a super hilarious comedian who's on the verge of hitting the big time. Unfortunately, your real name is "David Daniel Kaminsky," and your handlers are demanding a stage name. Which stage name works best?

    A) Danny Kaye

    B) Gummo Marx

    C) Moms Mabley

    D) Tim Kazurinsky

    E) Danny the "Kamino" of comedy

24. CLASSIFICATION QUIZ:

    If you've decided to be the kind of comic who gets his own sitcom, hosts *SNL,* and appears on magazine covers, which type of comedian should you be?

    A) cigar comedian

    B) moustache comedian

    C) glasses comedian

    D) gross-out comedian

    E) awful comedian

25. The movie *Airplane!,* although it inspired many rip-offs (*Scary Movie, My Big Fat Independent Movie, Date Movie*), was actually the only film in this genre to be truly funny. True or false?

26. Repeating a variation of the same joke 3 times within a performance is an example of:

    A) the rule of 3s

    B) a runner

    C) the callback

    D) overkill

27. A "charming asshole" has license to:

    A) insult everyone

    B) defy the rules

C) get what he wants

D) fuck the dean's wife

E) win

F) all of it

28. If you repeat popular catchphrases to garner laughs and popularity, you are considered:

A) funny

B) lame

C) "with it"

D) the living dead

29. FILL IN A BLANK:

Sid Caesar first shot to fame with his hilarious _____ routine.

A) war-movie routine

B) 7 dirty words routine

C) Sledge-o-matic routine

D) "Ya' doesn't has to call me Ray" routine

30. Jackie Mason is a Jew. True or false?

31. Who is not a "crazy hair" comedian?

A) Carrot Top

B) Harpo Marx

C) Lyle Waggoner

D) Gallagher 2

32. A funny complaint letter should be read by:

A) an insulted Englishman

B) a regular Joe

C) bishop or leader of religious group

D) a transvestite or anyone with lisp

E) a naked man

33. Steve Allen didn't think the word "fuck" was funny.
    True or false?

34. YOU'RE THE FOIL:
    You are a respectable bank president dining in an 8-star
    restaurant. The waiter mistakenly shits on your plate
    (gangsters forced him to). What is the proper reaction?

    A) a double take
    B) a spit take
    C) an unlimited take
    D) say "oy vey!"
    E) after initial outrage, smell excrement as if to say
       "hey, not bad!"
    F) break the 4th wall
    G) cross your eyes

35. You've written a joke that is only "borderline funny."
    In performance, which one will help "knock it out of the
    park"?

    A) shouting
    B) turn it into a catchphrase
    C) excessive vomiting
    D) delivered by precocious child
    E) drop trou and reveal underwear

36. Who is not a "utility comedian"?

    A) Dan Aykroyd
    B) Phil Hartman
    C) Will Ferrell
    D) Anthony Michael Hall

37. Which cartoon studio had the funniest sound effects
    library?

    A) Warner Bros.
    B) Hanna Barbara
    C) Filmation
    D) Max Fleischer Studios

38. Which film was the better rip-off of *It's a Mad, Mad, Mad, Mad World*?

   A) *Scavenger Hunt*
   B) *Rat Race*
   C) *Independence Day*
   D) *Schindler's List*

39. Which movie-inspired-by-an-*SNL*-character should never have been made?

   A) *The Blues Brothers 2000*
   B) *It's Pat: The Movie*
   C) *The Jimmy Fallon Cracks Up Movie*
   D) *The Coneheads*
   E) they're all totally worth it

40. Which one was never a movie-inspired-by-an-*SNL*-character?

   A) *The Goat-Boy Movie*
   B) *The Horatio Sanz Cracks-up Movie*
   C) *Da Bears!: Da Movie*
   D) *The Charles Rocket Saying "Fuck" Movie*
   E) thank Christ, all of them

41. FANTASY WORLD:
   If Jay Leno never existed, which comic should have, by rights, taken over the *Tonight Show* when Johnny left?
   A) David Letterman
   B) a 5-year-old Dane Cook
   C) Magic Johnson
   D) Wayland Flowers & Madam

42. Whose "writers' room" was the craziest?

   A) *Your Show of Shows*
   B) *Saturday Night Live* 1984-85
   C) *The Smothers Brothers Comedy Hour*
   D) *Lidsville*

43. Which is the best example of a comedian who "forgot the bit" (i.e. gave up what made them funny in the first place)?

A) the Unknown Comic performing without the bag
B) Joe Piscopo becoming muscle-bound
C) Robin Williams becoming a serious actor
D) John Belushi dying

44. The funniest "retard movie" is:

A) *I Am Sam*
B) *The Other Sister*
C) *Bill* (the Mickey Rooney one)
D) *The House of D*
E) *David And Lisa*
F) *Door To Door*
G) *Riding The Bus With My Sister*

EXTRA-CREDIT QUESTION!

Robin Williams and Rosie O'Donnell are just two of the many comedians who have portrayed "special" people in very serious films. Which one of the following comics do you think is also "ready" for this brave challenge?

A) Willie Tyler and Lester
B) Jimmy Kimmel
C) Robin Williams again
D) Cedric the Entertainer
F) Yahoo Serious

END OF TEST. PENCILS DOWN.

HOW DO YOU THINK YOU DID? (*ANSWERS IN NEXT VOLUME.*)

HISTORICAL... HYSTERICAL!

More info for your "MENTAL FUN-O-DEX."
There's nothing cooler than someone who can
memorize funny bits from funny movies!

SOME CLASSIC FUNNY MOVIES THAT YOU SHOULD HAVE SEEN BY NOW. IF YOU HAVEN'T, PLEASE RENT/BUY THE DVD ASAP.

Some **Comedy By the Numbers®** numbers are used in these films to great effect!

Blazing Saddles	#2, 5, 10, 14, 24, 27, 30, 40, 43, 47, 54, 63, 65, 66, 77, 79, 83, 85, 100, 105, 110, 113, 136, 139, 151, 158, 162
The Jerk	#2, 3, 5, 8, 10, 21, 23, 31, 35, 44, 49, 50, 58, 68, 79, 94, 110, 113, 118, 137, 156, 159, 169
Annie Hall	#63
Bananas	#63
This is Spinal Tap	#3, 10, 12, 21, 36, 45, 50, 56, 60, 69, 72, 78, 87, 89, 99, 125, 127, 130, 138, 162, 168
Love and Death	#26, #63
Lost in America	#3, 5, 13, 28, 41, 59, 61,62, 63,64, 114, 116, 124, 130, 142, 155, 165, 169
Dr. Strangelove	#2, 3, 7, 10, 24, 25, 31, 38, 44, 47, 49, 50, 58, 62, 65, 66, 73, 81, 91, 103, 104, 117, 125, 155, 162
Animal House	#2, 5, 10, 14, 21, 24, 30, 34, 37, 51, 61, 65, 68, 72, 91, 102, 113, 118, 134, 141, 144, 155, 162
Kentucky Fried Movie	#1-169
Slap Shot	#2, 3, 9, 23, 38, 39, 40, 47, 49, 50, 65, 89, 94, 113, 122, 123, 129, 144, 152, 162
Some Like It Hot	#30, 55, 59, 65, 79, 107, 144 - mostly 107 for laughs
The Producers	#2, 10, 24, 28, 32, 44, 47, 50, 56, 57, 61, 63, 81, 92, 116, 139, 140-146, 162, 169
Cheech & Chong: Up in Smoke	#34, 47
M*A*S*H	#2, 3, 5, 10, 15, 25, 30, 34, 40, 41, 45, 62, 66, 69, 73, 81, 85, 94, 102, 114, 119, 140, 141, 160, 166, 169

The Cocoanuts, Animal Crackers, Duck Soup, Horse Feathers, Monkey Business, A Night at the Opera, A Day at the Races, ...oh, hell, ALL the Marx Bros. movies!   #2, 3, 5, 7, 10, 21, 28, 30, 31, 37, 41, 43, 44, 47, 49, 50, 51, 54, 55, 59, 60, 62, 63, 68, 74, 75, 76, 79, 81, 85, 89, 91, 98, 99, 100, 101, 108, 114, 116, 119, 122, 124, 125, 129, 130, 132, 133-153, 156, 157, 162, 168, 169

This list goes on and on, but we stopped here – what do you think, we're made of paper?!

BIBLIOGRAPHY

Unlike a lot of other authors (Gore Vidal!), we are more than happy to recommend the "competition" to you. If you learn more from these books than we've taught you, we'll give you double your free back! Now, it's been "said" that the cornerstone (literally!) of any good comedy library is *Uncle Milton's Joke and Josh Compendium: 30,000 Laughs for all occasions!*. But when 30 thou' ain't enough, we recommend you check your local library for some of the following titter-inducing tomes:

- *The Three Stooges 3 Jokes*
- Carrot Top's *324 Things That Can Be Other Things*
- Howie Mandel's *89 Yelps and Spazz-isms*
- *39 General Topics for Alternative Comedy*
- Howard Stern's *567 Lowest Common Denominators*
- Tim Boltor's *Mastering the Toast: 568 Official Toastmaster Rules and Strictures*
- Alec Whimples' *7,000 Dry English Ripostes and LollyGags*
- Robert Benchley's *Your Very Own Algonquin Roundtable* home kit
- *1001 How Many Y'all's White Trash Assholes Like Me?* by T. Boogie Dougal
- Foster Brooks' *345 Drunk-isms*
- Phyllis Diller's *1 Way to be Kooky For Money*
- Byron Allen's *456 Mildly Comical Interjections*
- Wayne Brady's *3456 "Look-At-Me's!"*
- *The Big Book of Jokes, Japes, Joshes, Ridicu-mention-ables, Laugh-aws, Chuckle-bringers, Whee-hees, and Yuk-bucklers,* by none other than Mr. Throw-It-Against-The-Wall himself, Mel Brooks!

SCIENTIFIC BACK-UP RESEARCH INFORMATION

The material contained within this book was specifically presented to focus groups at some of the country's hottest comedy clubs. It was determined through scientific analysis that these randomly selected people reflect your exact comedic sensibilities and life goals. You can trust them. They all really really liked this stuff. Those clubs are:

- Double Overz (*Michigan*)
- The Komedy Storr (*Los Angeles*)
- Milk Thru Your Noze (*Baltimore*)
- yUk hUt – where "U" are funny (*Salt Lake City*)
- Ha Ha Ha Ha Hee Hee Hoo Hoo Har Har Ohhh That Was Funny's! – Thursdays only (*Indianapolis*)
- Lafff Traxxx – featuring the country's first individual comedy porn booths for a quarter (*San Francisco*)
- The Holocaust Museum Café – the big one (*Washington*)
- Chuckle Shack (*Kokomo*)
- Yes And… I'll have a Drink (*Raleigh, NC – in the back of a Great American PayDay Money4U store*)

AND HERE'S A COPY OF MY CERTIFICATE OF RITUAL CIRCUMCISION THAT I'VE BEEN CARRYING AROUND IN MY WALLET EVER SINCE MY MOTHER FOUND A COPY OF IT AND SHOWED IT TO ME.

(My original name was Gary Ruderman and not Gary Rudoren, but both of us have the same penis)

DON'T PUT THE BOOK DOWN JUST YET

In this age of electronic correspondence, we thought we'd go OLD SCHOOL (#89) and make it easier for you to send us a note of thanks and congratulations the old-fashioned way. That's why we've purposefully taken 39 cents off the suggested retail price of the book: to compensate you for the stamp your fan letter will require. We didn't have the budget to supply envelopes, but I'm sure your boss won't mind if you borrow one from work.

We've also written an outline letter to make it even easier for you to acknowledge us and our contribution toward your new found success. That's the attached letter, just below the dotted line.

That's it – thanks in advance for your thanks!

Your new friends,

Gary & Eric

(By the time you've finished our book, you should be on a first-name basis with us.)

MAIL TO
849 Valencia St
San Francisco, CA 94110

- (cut here) -

Dear Eric & Gary,

Oh, my _____! I just finished reading COMEDY BY THE NUMBERS© and it has _____ my life! I wanted to take the time to write you to acknowledge how great both of you _____.

I'm not the kind of person who normally writes a letter like this. But when I read COMEDY BY THE NUMBERS©, I felt like you were talking directly to me! Your magical words have given me the inspiration to pursue that career in comedy or even try to be popular, instead of staying home to masturbate to _____. Wish me luck!

If you're ever in my hometown of _____, _____, I hope you'll call me at _____ to see if we can get together! Drinks are on me!

Thanks again for your vision,

_____

PS - I almost forgot! My favorite COMEDY number is _____!

PPS - Do you mind if I tell you my best original idea for a commercial hit comedy film? Here goes… _____
_____
_____
_____! Please let me know what you think of this unsolicited idea! I'll consider this letter with my signature a legal waiver allowing you to use my idea in some way if that helps you! Hey, I owe you one!

LAST WORDS AND HUMBLE THANKS

The authors would especially like to thank...

OUR FIRST SUPPORTERS, OUR EDITORS, AND THE PEOPLE WITHOUT WHOM THIS BOOK JUST DOESN'T GET DONE: Naomi Odenkirk and Bob Odenkirk.

AND THEN BOB AND NAOMI SHOWED SOME OF THE BOOK TO THESE GUYS, WHO COULDN'T HAVE BEEN MORE ENTHUSI-ASTIC, SUPPORTIVE, TALENTED, AND COOL AS READERS AND EDITORS: Dave Eggers and Eli Horowitz.

SOME OF THE FOLK WHO, OVER THE YEARS, WE COLLABO-RATED WITH AND/OR STOLE FROM AND WHO WE HOPE WILL CONSIDER THIS HEARTFELT THANKS AS "PAYMENT": Mike Monterastelli; Matt Walsh (for the numbers); Jay Johnston; Jeff Fox at Barracuda Magazine; Scot Robinson; Bill Chott; Madeline Long; Kate Flannery; Susan Messing; Pat Walsh; Sheldon Patinkin; Norm Holly; Mick Napier; David Cross; Beer Shark Mice; Paget Brewster; Anne-Marie Rounkle; Pat Healy; Paul F. Tompkins; Matt Besser; Peter Alberts, Steve Cowdrey; Tony Stavish; Dan Wachtel; Mike Berson; Joe Lamirand; Paul Bickel; Curt Clevenger; Tim Don Perkins; Mike Hollander; C.J. Arabia; Karen Kilgariff; The Gnarlers; eyeclops; Robin Aldrich; Ken Manthey; Chris Gore; Jason Pardo; all at Odenkirk Talent Mgmt; all at the Dickie Bell Twist Dance Party; Jordan Bass, Angela Petrella, Jory John, Chris Lindgren, and all at McSweeney's; all at the Annoyance Theatre; all at the UCB Theatres (both); James Grace and the IO West; All at Mr. Show; all at Film Threat; Sid and Eleanore Schecter; Jo and Mildred Bakstad; Mark Sutton, Jim Carrane, Jennifer Estlin, David Summers, Dick Costolo, Lyn Pusztai, Jim Plunkard, Ray Hartshorne, Sophie Bidek, Christina Musilek, Dave Goetsch, Jen Wang, Tyrone Finch, AJ Jacobs, anyone we forgot, and someone we won't forget, Martin deMaat.

GARY'S EXTRA-SPECIAL THANKS: Arlene & Howard Ruderman and the whole extended family... and especially Jodi, yes, especially Jodi.

ERIC'S EXTRA-SPECIAL THANKS: Chris and Kari Bentz; Jerry Hoffman.

GARY & ERIC ALSO WANTED TO THANK: Each other.

PHOTOS CREDITS THAT WE WANTED TO MENTION: Red Sandwich photos by Paget Brewster, yes THE Paget Brewster; Chic Tongue photo by Anne-Marie Rounkle; Goombahs! photo by Ken Manthey, yes THE Ken Manthey.

ABOUT THE AUTHORS

Thank you for making it all the way to the back of the book! Good job! As a reward, here's some info on us.

ABOUT ERIC HOFFMAN

Eric Hoffman (aka Eric Von Hoffman) was a writer on HBO's *Mr. Show with Bob and David*. He has acted in the films *My Big Fat Independent Movie*, *Mullitt!*, and *The Brothers Solomon*. And he is one half of the comedy team "The Snüz Brothers." He is also a Ducky Award-winning director of the Annoyance Theatre's show *Goombahs!* Eric enjoyed writing this book.

ABOUT GARY RUDOREN

The formerly named Gary Ruderman has juggled a variety of careers over the years as a writer, director, actor, photographer, set designer and architect. He is an ensemble member of the Annoyance Theatre in Chicago, where he created dozens of plays. His one-man serial killer play *So, I Killed A Few People...* has been performed on several continents and was published in the anthology *Plays and Playwrights for the New Millennium*. **Comedy By The Numbers** sprang from his collaboration with Eric on the Annoyance comedy hit *The Idiotic Death of Two Fools*. Not to be outdone, he has won several coveted Duckies and also enjoyed writing this book.

DID YOU KNOW?

Much like Thomas Payne, the authors created this book in the revolutionary "pamphlet" form first!

LET'S NOT CALL THIS THE END, OUR FRIEND... TILL WE MEET AGAIN IN THE POSSIBLE SEQUEL

(which, if you remember from the beginning of the book, is dependent upon you purchasing multiple copies of this fine product for friends or whomever).